Praise for *The Power of Thanks*

"The best endorsement for *The Power of Thanks* is simple 'thanks.' Thanks for a well written, insightful, useful, and timely book on how leaders can create abundant cultures that deliver employee and company results."

> —Dave Ulrich, Rensis Likert Collegiate Professor of Business Administration, University of Michigan; Partner the RBL Group

"Thank you, Eric Mosley and Derek Irvine for providing practitioners with both the practical and empirical value of appreciation in your book, *The Power of Thanks*. Through their mix of case studies, anecdotes, and examples, they underscore the role of social recognition in building culture and driving sustainable business performance. Given that – by definition – appreciation is "…an ability to understand the worth, quality, or importance of something," Eric and Derek have contributed immeasurably to the appreciation of the importance of others' use of a simple, but significant phrase: "Thank you.'"

> —Mark Berry, Vice President of People Insights, ConAgra Foods

"A very readable, practical and engaging primer on building a culture of recognition. Indispensable for the practising HR leader."

> —Hayagreeva Rao, Atholl McBean Professor of Organizational Behavior, Graduate School of Business, Stanford University

"All people, in all levels, will benefit from reading this book. It is a reminder that gratitude in the workplace is a critical driver for success – for businesses large and small. Not only does it boost employee morale, it fuels higher levels of performance by making your culture a great one."

> —Rieva Lesonsky, CEO of GrowBiz Media and former Editorial Director of *Entrepreneur* Magazine

"This book is the equivalent of getting tutored by a world-class corporate culture coach. Its clear, concise, and often eye-opening insight is a road map toward a happier and more productive workforce."

> —John Hollon, Vice President of Editorial, TLNT.com, and the former Editor of *Workforce Management* magazine

"The simple act of saying thank you, and doing it often, is a brilliant way to bring humanity into the work experience. This book provides tangible and simple ways to make gratitude a priority when interacting with colleagues, creating work environments that are richer, more productive and frankly more fun."

> —Tim Leberecht, author of *The Business Romantic* and CMO of NBBJ

THE
POWER
OF
THANKS

THE
POWER
OF
THANKS

How Social Recognition Empowers Employees and Creates a Best Place to Work

ERIC MOSLEY
and
DEREK IRVINE

New York   Chicago   San Francisco   Lisbon   London   Madrid
Mexico City   Milan   New Delhi   San Juan   Seoul
Singapore   Sydney   Toronto

2 3 4 5 6 7 8 9 0   DOC/DOC   1 9 8 7 6 5

ISBN   978-0-07-183840-5
MHID 0-07-183840-6

e-ISBN   978-0-07-183841-2
e-MHID 0-07-183841-4

McGraw-Hill Education books are available at special quantity discounts to use as premiums and sales promotions or for use in corporate training programs. To contact a representative, please e-mail us at bulksales@mheducation.com.

CONTENTS

PREFACE

The ideas in this book represent 15+ years of creating better work environments. Our vision at Globoforce is to help build the best, most admired workplaces around the world, starting with our own.

There are many strategies and books on how to accomplish this—and many of them have a lot of merit and value to today's business and HR leaders. Our approach is a bit different, as we believe that the foundation of a great workplace starts with the power of thanks and recognition. When employees feel appreciated, they not only work harder, they trust each other and their leaders more. It creates lasting bonds between employees that infuse this trust into all areas of the business. After all, people are people. Many become friends with their coworkers. Many have worked with their coworkers at previous companies. People work better and harder when they have a level of trust with their colleagues. Building a culture of recognition and positivity is the key ingredient needed for relationships to thrive and for trust to be possible.

At Globoforce, our journey toward creating a culture of recognition started with our values. Our values drive every aspect of our work and our success. For us, Imagination + Determination = Innovation. That innovation was the impetus for us looking at employee recognition in a new way—for recreating employee recognition for a modern workforce and making it a business imperative. We're fortunate to have many believers along that journey with us—our customers. Early in our company's history, we had many "early adopters" to the new vision of recognition. These companies (many of whom are included in this book) were true pioneers. They saw an opportunity to disrupt the thinking of what recognition meant and what it could mean for their business. And today, many of these same human resources (HR) leaders are in higher, more prominent roles in their company because of their foresight and belief in the power of thanks and recognition.

Our customers are executives, managers, and human resources professionals in organizations ranging from domestic manufacturing to globally distributed technology leaders. Across many industries and cultures, they all share the challenge of building and sustaining a winning workforce. You probably have that challenge, too. To succeed, you need motivated, engaged, and energized employees who understand your mission and are focused on achieving it. You need to attract great employees in the first place, help people reach their fullest potential, and form innovative teams that produce results and retain the best, all while holding the line on your human capital budget. Above all, you need to unite a diverse and far-flung company of individuals in a culture of shared values and common purpose.

These are not easy challenges to meet. Yet our customers do so every day, and along the way they share their experiences, insights, and questions with us. Creating human capital solutions for businesses as different as nanotechnology, civil engineering, and hotel management has given us a unique understanding of how company culture drives performance and how direct, authentic human appreciation drives culture.

Throughout the years we have developed a system of practices and technologies we call *Social Recognition*®, which we define in the first pages of this book.

Here's what you'll find in *The Power of Thanks*:

You will learn how a "Positivity Dominated Workplace" creates and maintains competitive advantage.

You will learn a data-driven, proven, and repeatable model for proactively managing culture. The model is built on foundations as well established as Abraham Maslow's Hierarchy of Needs and Peter Drucker's analysis of the relative power of culture and strategy paired with innovations for today's workforce.

You will find a road map for social recognition, enabling you to implement a program in a matter of weeks across a large enterprise, in many languages, and on any continent.

You will find a complete discussion of social recognition's return on investment and models for determining its value in your company before you get started. (Our HR customers have learned to prove the value of recognition to the C-Suite in advance.)

Along the way, you'll hear from our customers, researchers, industry analysts, management gurus, and human capital experts, all sharing their wisdom as they strive to improve the most important part of any company—the people living its mission day by day.

Why are we the people to tell you this?

Globoforce reinvented employee recognition, which hadn't changed much since the gold-watch days of our grandparents. We saw the opportunity to harness the power of thanks in a completely different way, not only because technology has changed, but also because of vast global changes in workforce management, including:

- The increasing power and mobility of the world's most talented employees
- The need to drive creativity, innovation, and accountability into every corner of the workplace
- The eagerness of employees of all kinds to share common values and common empowerment in a fast-changing work environment
- The realization that employee engagement is the key metric of effectiveness in human capital management
- The worldwide adoption of mobile, social, and 24/7 communications
- Pervasive software-as-a-service (SaaS) product design

And perhaps most exciting of all, we found the capacity of modern data analysis to unlock hidden insights. Recognizing patterns in something as simple and genuine as one person showing appreciation for another is a profound business advantage. Multiplied in a large organization by thousands of such moments, and captured in advanced data models, the Power of Thanks has the ability not only to create motivation and good feeling, but also to uncover the hidden currents and networks of a company—the social architecture that defines an organization far more accurately than an organization chart. There is immense power when you unleash real human relationships within a company.

At Globoforce we are privileged to bring home the solutions we create for our customers, and our own social recognition practice is a key advantage for what was once a small company taking on the long-established competitors in our field. How are we doing on our vision? Globoforce was named as one of the 25 "Best Places to Work" in the United States and one of the top 50 workplaces in all of Europe. We practice what we preach because we know it works.

And it works for our customers, too. A social recognition practice, enabling both goodwill and great insight, is more than theory. The proof of our practice is in the success of our customers, whose stories open each chapter. Many of them are on the lists of the best, most admired workplaces in the world. And for them, that great workplace starts with having a culture of recognition that empowers and energizes all employees.

Many of our customers had different specific goals. But the common thread for all of them was wanting to build a better workplace for their employees—giving them an environment where they're more engaged and energized.

All of them started their recognition journey by asking a lot of questions. We hope this book answers some of yours.

ACKNOWLEDGEMENT

Before we begin, working within our own culture of recognition, now is the time to call out the much appreciated and valuable contributions made by many people to this book.

First off, our special thanks goes to Kevin Mullins, Lynette Silva, and Doug Hardy for helping us with the production of this book. We laughed a lot, had some fun, but during tough decision times (which would have sunk less experienced folks), their total professionalism helped carry us through smoothly. All three have been pivotal contributors to this book in various ways. We also greatly appreciate the contributions of Charlie Ungashick, Jessica Bergeron, Pam Goodwin, and Darcy Jacobsen.

A huge call-out goes to our customers. Without them and their enthusiastic support for everything we in Globoforce have been doing over the past decade, none of this would have been possible. It's particularly gratifying for us when we see our customers achieve success across their organizations through the power of thanks; they then go on to become strong advocates and champions for social recognition. We have also learned a great deal from our customers. We appreciate immensely your continued enthusiasm for what is now a revolution in the thinking about social recognition, company culture, and the power of thanks. A particular call out to those who participated in this book: JetBlue, IHG, Intuit, Baker Hughes, Symantec, The Hershey Company, Bechtel, ConAgra Foods, and IM Flash.

And finally, to each and every employee of Globoforce, your actions everyday are what make our company special, what brings to life our thinking. We never forget that without our collective focus on our own values and on what we need to do to succeed, none of this would be possible. This book is dedicated to you.

Introduction – The Power of Thanks

There is incredible power in the word *Thanks*.

When people are thanked for a job well done, they feel a sense of purpose. They love their work. They are inspired to do even better. They have a tremendous sense of loyalty to their employer. And every day, they come to work looking for new ways to do more to help the company surpass its goals.

For modern businesses today, *thanks* is not only a new way to drive employee performance. Thanks is a unifying force that gets business results, inspires great workplaces, creates the right culture, and helps to secure—even create—a competitive advantage.

A Culture of Recognition

Culture is the heart and soul of any organization. Culture drives competitive advantage. Culture is powerful, pervasive, and enduring. In a business world abundant with resources of technology, capital, management talent, and good ideas, culture makes the difference between excellence and mediocrity, between success and failure.

Culture is also widely misunderstood, abused, and neglected. Some leaders who pride themselves in active management of areas like finance and technology treat culture management as a matter of displaying a wordy mission statement on the lobby wall. Others, aware that culture is critical to success, assume it requires little more than talking about company values at the annual sales meeting. And some leaders believe culture is the unmanageable "magic" that happens when you get the right people in the right seats and leave them alone.

We at Globoforce are in the "Thanks" business, using the power of thanks to proactively manage culture—yes, *manage* it. Culture can be managed scientifically, with rigorous and authentic processes. An organization's culture can be learned, encouraged, ingrained, and applied to every business process, in many forms and across all parts of the organization. Applied correctly, culture management through proven practices we call social recognition drive measurable improvements in operating margins, income, and customer satisfaction. Our customers know this is true; they've done it.

Social recognition creates new value in the forms of goodwill, loyalty, employee engagement, and personal meaning. That value brings tangible benefits such as greater profits and also drives strategic objectives of a modern organization such as corporate social responsibility. The technology supporting social recognition also serves as a diagnostic tool of organizational health. As we shall see, it identifies the hidden strengths (and weaknesses) of a company's operations at every level.

Achieving true recognition success happens through a process we call the social recognition journey. Companies start out with small, intuitive steps like publicly giving thanks for great performance. This *tactical recognition* is the most common form of recognition—the plaque on the cubicle wall and a mention in the company monthly e-mail. It's very basic, the equivalent of placing a "like" notice on a Facebook page. Most companies are familiar with this and practice it (though often as an afterthought).

The next step in the recognition journey is *enterprise recognition*, which requires applying a bit more structure and resources to a recognition program across the entire organization. This is where many recognition programs include cash or other awards, and HR departments track the recognition program. Enterprise recognition means propagating best practices across the company, around the world, often to consolidate efforts enterprise-wide. It gives better results than tactical recognition because it's managed in a quantifiable and consistent way. And most organizations on the recognition journey stop there.

Strategic recognition is a significant step forward because it aligns the entire program, from funding recognition awards to defined reasons for recognition to capturing the data that a program can provide to strategic goals. Strategic recognition is on a par with first-rate financial controls or just-in-time procurement policies. No longer a nice-to-have, it is the technology that enables a host of strategic goals, just as financial practices and technology know-how enable strategic goals.

Social recognition is the mass mobilization of all employees that's pivotal to unleashing the full power of recognition. Using the benefit of new social technologies, social recognition gives employees a voice to say *Thanks!* . . . and say it often. It channels the positivity of thanks to continuously reinforce the values at the heart of company culture. Through many positive feedback moments, social recognition deepens the resolve of an organization to celebrate what's being done right, every day, everywhere. Social recognition also creates a paradigm shift from old-school thinking that believes gratitude and rewards only come from the top down. In social recognition (just as in social networks like TripAdvisor and Amazon's "star ratings" system), positive feedback and thanks are truly sourced from the wide "crowd" that is your employee base. When done with real employee enablement and genuineness, it is powerful stuff!

Executive Insight

"I really focus on the values and the standards of the organization. What are the expected behaviors? How do we want to treat each other? How do we want to act? What do we want to do about transparency? How can we have a safe environment where we really know what's going on?"

—Alan R. Mulally, former president and CEO of Ford Motor Company[1]

At Globoforce, we've seen the business results of taking the recognition journey, and our customers show us the many ways social recognition improves performance:

- At JetBlue, social recognition supports the culture that leaders believe is their company's greatest competitive advantage in a very competitive business.
- At IHG (InterContinental Hotels Group), social recognition helps inspire global employees to become "BrandHearted Heroes," delivering great service day in, day out.
- At Intuit, social recognition enables simple human emotions like appreciation and gratitude to inspire above-and-beyond results.
- At Baker Hughes, HR and executives are using social recognition to motivate and retain far-flung workers who might otherwise be isolated (on an oil rig in the Gulf, for example).
- At Symantec, the software leader evolved its social recognition practice to better manage a "culture of cultures" arising through many mergers.
- The Hershey Company enables 13,000 employees around the globe to recognize great performance anytime, anywhere—using a computer or a mobile app.
- Engineering and construction giant Bechtel is proud of being a very traditional company, but it has embraced data-driven, peer-to-peer social recognition from the construction site to the C-suite.
- At ConAgra Foods, social recognition is combined with demographic data to predict previously unknowable business risks like attrition.
- Tech company IM Flash uses the data from its social recognition program to measure company culture and connect it to business outcomes.

Is It Time to Manage Your Culture?

Every organization has a culture, whether it's the culture the leadership wants or the one that has come to exist through inertia and management neglect. Businesses are societies, and society and culture are inseparable. Managing your company's culture—acknowledging where it is today and taking it where you want it to be—is critical to achieving your strategic objectives, as critical as managing your company's cash flow.

The work of culture management through social recognition begins with understanding the true nature of a company's culture. When we evaluate the culture of our customers' workplaces, we ask:

- Is your organization's culture deliberately managed or left to develop by accident?
- Is your culture aligned to and supportive of your company values?
- Does your culture contribute every day to your strategic goals or hinder them?
- Can every employee, at any level, describe the authentic culture of your company?
- Who feels they own your culture? HR? Or all employees?
- And most important—can you prove your answers to these questions are correct?

This book serves as a guide for business leaders to harness the power of thanks and culture. Think of the hallmarks of your culture—your company values. These statements of desired behaviors and actions suggest and reinforce your culture. But how do you make your values real to every employee so employees apply them to everyday tasks? Social recognition, implemented correctly and strategically, is your most powerful way to manage, inspire, encourage, and measure the values you have chosen for your organization.

In this book we'll teach you how the practice of social recognition achieves these goals. We'll explain a five-level, progressive model of culture management; we'll build on foundations of management science, research, and our experience implementing recognition at leading corporations including Intuit, JetBlue, IHG, Symantec, ConAgra Foods, and many more. The book is organized into three parts:

Part 1—Understanding Organizational Culture

We will describe the behaviors found in an effective culture and how transactional factors among people such as appreciation, recognition, and respect benefit all employees individually and inspire the most productive attitudes and behaviors.

Chapter 1: The Rise of Company Culture

This chapter explains how culture drives core values deep into an organization, and why culture is the defining driver of today's business environment.

Chapter 2: The People-First Workplace

Why does appreciation matter to a company's bottom line? This chapter demonstrates how the power of thanks works with individual employees and across an organization to create, encourage, and manage a chosen culture. We'll show how and why recognition enables employees and organizations to reach their fullest potential, and we'll discuss the latest research confirming an old-fashioned idea: that happiness at work benefits organizations of all kinds.

Chapter 3: Appreciation, Gratitude, and Employee Engagement

Management studies and social science create a progressive framework for understanding why giving and receiving appreciation is not only beneficial but vital to a well-functioning organization. Many sources, from Maslow's famous hierarchy of psychological needs to McKinsey's research about employee engagement, suggest a model for moving culture forward.

Part 2—Understanding Social Recognition

Social recognition is a set of practices to manage company culture. Before planning a social recognition program, everyone involved needs to understand how it works and where it is going in the coming decade.

Chapter 4: Setting a Purpose and a Vision

Leadership means telling the world why a company exists—its purpose—and describing a vision for how that purpose will be achieved. Of course, this includes the strategy and tactics for delivering products and services to market. Critically, it also includes the *way* in which those results will be achieved—the underlying acceptable behaviors and environment to deliver on the business plan: in other words, the company's culture. Strategically implemented recognition moves people toward that vision, and it is achieved through a social architecture that enables individuals to contribute to that progress through their work.

Chapter 5: The Evolution and Reinvention of Recognition

This chapter examines the breakthrough concepts that move recognition from a "nice to have" benefit to an invaluable practice fully integrated with global management systems. We'll share a model of how recognition progresses from individual moments of appreciation and thanks to an enterprise-wide and socially empowered practice.

Chapter 6: Social, Mobile, and 24/7

Workforce habits and employee behavior are changing faster today than at any time in the past. The impact of online social behavior, mobile technology, and a cultural shift toward 24/7 connectivity is changing interaction across geographies, generations, and hierarchies. We'll show how recognition fits in this new work paradigm.

Part 3—Putting Social Recognition into Practice

Acknowledging culture's role in the workplace and social recognition's role in culture management, Part 3 is a blueprint for putting recognition into practice following several essential principles. As part of implementing social recognition, Part 3 also described the key business impacts of recognition beyond managing culture.

Chapter 7: Building a Social Recognition Framework

This chapter outlines a step-by-step plan for implementing social recognition in your organization, with strategies and key practices that will improve your culture and results.

Chapter 8: Driving ROI and Business Results

Any recognition program worthy of the name should deliver measurable return on investment. In addition to improving the bottom line, recognition advances key HR goals such as employment branding, becoming a great place for people to work, increasing employee engagement and energy, and boosting retention.

Chapter 9: How Social Recognition Impacts HR

Social recognition's impact radiates outward to key executive concerns such as health and wellness, safety initiatives, change management, performance reviews, and predictive workforce analytics. We will show how to bolster each of these practices using the benefits of recognition, from the concrete (workforce analytics) to the ephemeral (employee goodwill).

This book represents the best thinking from the best-performing organizations on culture, employee engagement, and the simple human truths underlying successful management practices. We'll share their wisdom in the text and in special comments we call "Expert Insights," along with cautionary observations from companies that ignored these truths at great cost. The best practices presented here can help you and your organization leverage the power of thanks to create a culture of recognition that drives performance, profits, pride, and a best place to work.

"Who Are You on the Recognition Journey?"

That's the first question we ask at the recognition workshops we run. Our customers typically have some understanding of recognition, but they are either disappointed with their programs or they sense most recognition practices are out of date. Before turning to Chapter 1, take a moment to consider where you are on the recognition journey.

Are you:

___ *A complete stranger.* You've heard of recognition but have no idea how to go about it. Turn the page and read the book to the end before starting out on the journey.

___ *An experienced traveler.* You've had a recognition program in place but think it can be better. Ask if you see recognition as a strategic practice as described in Part 2.

___ *A time traveler.* It's 2014, but you're practicing recognition as if it were 1974. If you see one more plaque or statuette or "thumbs up!" badge, you'll suspect you're in a Dilbert® cartoon. Glance at Chapter 5 first, and imagine that your organization can fast-forward to the present using social recognition.

___ *A fast-lane cruiser.* You love technology and you're looking to leverage innovations like social media to energize your workforce. Skim Chapter 6 first; you'll see how to harness tectonic movements in culture and communications.

___ *An expedition leader.* You're a leader in HR or strategy tasked with increasing engagement, energy, and alignment. Take a quick look at Chapter 8, and decide what strategic goals you want to bolster with recognition. Then dive in (and share this book's message with the rest of your company's C-suite).

PART 1
UNDERSTANDING
ORGANIZATIONAL
CULTURE

1 | The Rise of Company Culture

Take everything that's not so great about air travel. Now think of ways to erase that through extraordinary customer service. "This was the mindset of our founders," says Michael Elliott, Senior Vice President of People at JetBlue, "when they created a small airline that is now a major player in the airline industry." Michael adds that the airline's mission has evolved to simply "inspire humanity" – which starts with treating JetBlue's employees, all of whom are called "crewmembers," with gratitude and kindness.

"Our five Values—Safety, Caring, Integrity, Passion and Fun—set us apart from the other guys," says Elliott. "Together, our crewmembers live these values, and in turn, make the JetBlue experience for our customers unmatchable. We strive to make it a down-to-earth company by hiring kind, hard-working crewmembers. Once they get here, we recognize and applaud them for being the heart of our brand. The Lift recognition program we developed with Globoforce enables us to reinforce our values among our 16,000 crewmembers while also showing them how much we appreciate that they are inspiring humanity one action at a time."

As they grow, most companies experience the same types of growing pains: costs, complexity, and revenue pressures. Elliott notes, "When you move from 1,000 to 16,000 crewmembers in just a few years, it is more difficult to recognize somebody for living the values, particularly in an operational climate where a lot of frontline crewmembers work at various airports in our network or 30,000 feet in the air."

But JetBlue has maintained its culture, and earned 10 consecutive honors from J.D. Power for the highest customer satisfaction among low-cost carriers in North America. That distinction attracts customers who return the love with loyalty.

"Knowing who delivers extraordinary customer service, who truly lives the values, and who contributes to the JetBlue culture is critical," Elliott concludes. "This provides a competitive advantage for us while keeping our customers happy and our company feeling small as we grow. If we can ensure we are recognizing crewmembers and inspiring them to keep up our exceptional level of service year after year, we can go anywhere."

* * *

The traditional model of employee loyalty rewarded by lifetime employment is long gone. The traditional method of top-down, command-driven productivity is also long gone. In their place, leading companies have discovered that company culture drives today's competitive advantage because it inspires the behaviors that create more value through work. Is your organization's culture inspiring employees to greater achievement?

A distinctive company culture starts with a clear vision, but vision alone doesn't establish and sustain a culture. That happens when the *values* inherent in a vision inspire *emotions* that then drive new *behaviors*. The right behaviors drive *change* (the right behaviors *are* change—of the right kind). And when the new behaviors are encouraged, they affirm the vision that started the cycle. It's the willingness to apply those values to everyday situations that drives a business vision forward.

Values powered by emotions lead to behaviors that make change. And change affirms the vision and the values. It's a virtuous cycle (Figure 1.1).

Emotions energize this virtuous cycle. When a manager recognizes an employee's behavior, personally and sincerely, both feel proud, gratified, and happy. There's a human connection that transcends the

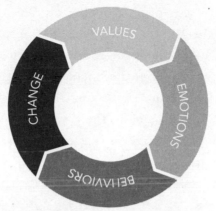

Figure 1.1 Virtuous cycle

immediate culture to create a shared bond. The power of this bond is stronger than you might think; indeed, it's the power that holds together great organizational cultures. Shared values, shared emotions, shared connections—these make organizations as much as they make civilizations.

The careers section of JetBlue's website declares, "JetBlue's culture was founded and built on five simple company values—Safety, Caring, Integrity, Fun and Passion—which we use as the basis for all our decisions, in work and life."

A healthy company culture is the most powerful way to find, build, and keep an engaged, high-performing workforce, which in turn is the only sustainable competitive advantage in today's global marketplace.

Technology can be acquired or imitated quickly; new strategy can be copied as soon as it's described in a business journal or blog; capital is available from more sources than ever; and in the world of Internet-based procurement, any large company can acquire goods and services for the best price. Even efficiency and productivity are so broadly understood that they offer only incremental advantage. Yesterday's differentiators are today's commodities. In today's rapidly changing and global marketplace, only an engaged workforce creates sustainable, defensible value.

Are you introducing new customer relationship management (CRM) software, or borrowing $100 million to build a new plant, or implementing a new strategic five-year plan? The commitment of your workforce will determine whether those technology, capital, or strategic investments succeed. And culture is the most powerful creator of commitment.

Peter Drucker, one of the greatest management thinkers of the 20th century, stated flatly, "Culture eats strategy for breakfast." Ford's COO Mark Fields placed that saying in the company's war room in 2006, and later we'll show why that belief was one of the main reasons Ford survived the auto-business meltdown of 2009.

What Is Culture?

Herb Kelleher, the legendary cofounder and chairman of Southwest Airlines, believed "Culture is what you do when people aren't looking." It's how employees behave when they step away from the power relationships in an organization and operate purely on instinct based on their own values. When those values are also shared with the organization, culture is nourished.

Writing in *Harvard Business Review*, Frances X. Frei and Anne Morriss commented, "Culture guides discretionary behavior, and it picks up where the employee handbook leaves off. Culture tells us how to respond to an unprecedented service request. It tells us whether to risk telling our bosses about our new ideas, and whether to surface or hide problems. Employees make hundreds of decisions on their own every day, and culture is our guide. Culture tells us what to do when the CEO isn't in the room, which is of course most of the time."[1]

An organization's culture is so much more than a slogan or poster. Culture is nothing less than the aggregate of tens of thousands of interactions and decisions every day. Leaders of great companies reinforce their values by rewarding and celebrating the behaviors that express those values.

The power of corporate culture was described a few years ago in the influential work of John P. Kotter and James L. Heskett. In *Corporate Culture and Performance* they wrote, "[Corporate cultures] can enable a group to take rapid and coordinated action against a competitor or for a customer."

> ## Executive Insight
>
> "Culture is a slow-growing tree. In the beginning it needs protection. But after a couple of decades the culture will be stronger than you are. You need to work with it, not against it. . . . Culture is a powerful but fragile thing. If you burn down the culture tree, it takes a long time to grow another one."
>
> —Wally Bock, *Three Star Leadership*[2]

Creating a culture means choosing a limited number of values that define the company as surely as its products or logo do, and then encouraging expression of those values in everyday behavior. No single set of values defines culture; greatness lies in authenticity. At Nike and GE, the culture includes keen competitive spirit—not just succeeding but *winning*. At Apple, designers will not put a power cord on a device that doesn't look beautiful and seamlessly aligned with the overall design of the product, because fabulous design and obsessive attention to detail are central to the Apple culture. Some firms, like Ryanair and Walmart, thrive on driving down costs, while others, like BMW and Rolex, focus on premium-priced engineering. If you care more about wringing the most value out of every single expenditure, you belong at Ryanair or Walmart, not BMW or Rolex.

What Fuels Culture?

Imagine that a large company decides that it needs to emphasize innovation (a common initiative these days). At this moment, all over the world, employees are trying innovations of all kinds. Sometimes it's a whole new product idea, and sometimes it's just a small improvement in an old process. People in customer service build a more customized database of replies to customer questions. People in operations refresh their Six Sigma certificates. People in marketing create an entertaining video about how to promote the company through social media, and all over the world, people in other departments watch the video and practice that new skill.

Now imagine that every time this happens, someone notices and expresses his or her thanks for the effort. There are little pieces of good-will happening between people. People are recognizing their colleagues, leaders, and employees for discretionary effort, for living the new company value: Innovation.

The spirit of innovation is becoming part of the company culture, and all of the positive reinforcement is inspiring greater engagement and greater emotional involvement in the staff. Senior leaders notice more discretionary work. People really listen to one another. Formerly timid employees speak up with new ideas. People who used to feel cynical about their chance of making a difference learn that they and their ideas matter, pushing themselves and others to do better. Everyone learns from the recognition received by others what "innovation" looks like in the daily work. People know what's expected of them and help to create a spirit of innovation everywhere.

As thanks and positive emotions are continuously linked to new behaviors, those new behaviors are sought out and multiply quickly, leading to profound culture change. This is the power of recognizing, celebrating, and reinforcing the right behaviors, attuned to company values. That's a good description of culture management.

Executive Insight

"I came to see, in my time at IBM, that culture isn't just one aspect of the game, it is the game. In the end, an organization is nothing more than the collective capacity of its people to create value."

—Louis V. Gerstner, former Chairman and CEO, IBM[3]

Culture in a Crisis

Culture saved Ford during the economic crisis of 2008 to 2009, when its competitors, General Motors and Chrysler, needed government bailouts to avoid shutting down. There were many reasons Ford stood in a stronger position than GM and Chrysler (including financial preparations and restructuring); principal among them were the moves then Chairman Alan Mulally made when he joined the company from Boeing in 2006. He gave Mark Fields, then COO (now CEO), the task of changing Ford's culture from the classic industrial-company combination of contention, distrust, and zero-sum negotiations (for me to win, you have to lose) with a set of values and behaviors called "One Ford." Those values and behaviors amount to a description of the Ford culture, and they include the following:[4]

- *Working together:* A belief in skilled and motivated people working together, and the expectation that everyone will respect, listen to, help, and appreciate others. Everyone's contribution is respected.
- *Modeling values:* Having a can-do, find-a-way attitude, and enjoying the journey and each other ("have fun—never at others' expense").
- *Delivering results:* Dealing positively with business realities—inspiring others, holding oneself and others responsible and accountable.

That last set of values is particularly interesting as a cultural note. Ford sees a culture of positivity, inspiration, and accountability not as a feel-good, nice-to-have part of the company but as essential to delivering results. One Ford includes tactical imperatives like "process discipline" and "technical excellence" (and those are also part of the culture)—but Mulally, who was brought in specifically to turn a troubled Ford around, emphasized the importance of everyone's personal commitment when he told *McKinsey Insights* in November 2013, "Some prefer to work in a different way. Ultimately, they will either adopt the Ford culture, or they will leave."[5]

Ford was hit hard by the Great Recession—sales dropped dramatically for every car company in 2008–2009—and Ford employees endured their share of economic pain. But armed with Drucker's admonition that culture eats strategy for breakfast, Ford's culture equipped it to come back quickly, with lower costs, better products, and a spirit of teamwork and shared sacrifice as well as shared rewards. In the five years from 2009 to 2014, the S&P 500 stock index doubled (as did the stock prices of Ford competitors like Toyota and Honda); General Motors emerged from bankruptcy, and its shares in late 2013 were about 10 percent above their 2009 value. Ford's share price in that five-year period rose more than 1,000 percent!

Culture is also at the heart of many business disasters, from the inability to change, innovate, or evolve (such as the "innovator's dilemma" described by bestselling management scholar Clayton Christensen) to cultures that stress business results at the expense of customers, society, and ethics (such as the shenanigans that led to the worldwide financial panic of 2008). Disgruntled employees, disappointed shareholders, and turned-off customers can feed a downward spiral from which a company never recovers.

The details change, but at the heart of great corporate successes and failures is a single observable phenomenon: the behaviors and values that constitute a company's culture largely determine its fate.

Culture as a Competitive Advantage

A strong organizational culture is a competitive advantage in its own right. It attracts talent. It promotes a winning spirit of optimism and energy. It bonds a diverse, global workforce of individuals into a common cause, language, and set of values. It earns the trust and goodwill of customers, which is important at all times and critical in a crisis.

Today's business world moves so quickly, and available information is so abundant, that speed and data overload combine to confound clear decision making. Shared values offer guidance through the storm—a true north for executives and employees making daily decisions in an ever-changing environment. That clarity contributes to making the right decisions and taking the right actions—a competitive advantage over organizations that don't have the true north of authentic, shared values.

MYTHBUSTER
Engaged Employees Are Long-Term Employees
It's a management truism that engaged employees are the greatest competitive advantage. Yet survey after survey, article after article, show that the majority of employees are ready and willing to jump ship. Towers Watson and WorldatWork found in 2013 that "Almost six in 10 companies report difficulty retaining critical-skill employees; similar proportions have difficulty retaining high-potential employees and top performers."[6]

What are you doing to show you appreciate your employees today and value their contribution over the long term?

If you are constantly talking about your culture, constantly seeking to teach people about your culture, talking culture *at* your people rather than pointing it out over and over as it is happening, it probably means the culture you want isn't fully part of your company's life. Culture must be something that truly is part of the DNA of the company, and the surest test is to observe whether employees' behavior reflects the desired culture without prompting.

When culture is alive and authentic, the employees understand it and are themselves responsible for it. Employees know what to do (tasks), how to do it (values-based behaviors), and why they should do it (impact on strategic company goals). Furthermore, they commit to the culture with loyalty and energy (emotions). When cultures are active and alive, even people applying for jobs will be able to articulate key elements of the company's culture. They'll reference it in interviews and tell you the culture is a big reason they're attracted to the company. (The employment website Glassdoor recently found that 90 percent of employees surveyed would consider leaving their current jobs if offered another role with a company that had an excellent reputation.)

This kind of clarity doesn't come from reading a brochure or glancing at the plaque in the lobby. It comes from steadily observing which behaviors are rewarded and why, day in and day out, in every division, corridor, and loading dock around the world.

Clarity and commitment are hard to achieve. An executive insight analysis by Bain & Company in 2006 found that even though business leaders know culture focuses and engages employees, only 15 percent of companies actually had high-performance cultures.[7] And again, this is a big reason for turnover. The Globoforce Fall 2012 Workforce Mood Tracker™ Survey found that 83 percent of employees departing a company rate culture as important in looking for a new job; only 45 percent of departing employees feel their old company had a positive culture.

Recognizing Culture with a Culture of Recognition

At a company like JetBlue, senior executives demonstrate and model their cultural values. In the early years of JetBlue, founder and CEO David Neeleman occasionally took the job of a cabin crewman, serving customers to demonstrate they came first, even before the CEO.[8]

When we talk to HR leaders at companies that really want to manage their cultures, they tell us, "Our CEO isn't giving this lip service. He (or she) has outright demanded this happen; this is the way we will behave at the company. We are moving ahead with improving and managing our culture, and everybody is paying attention."

The CEO and HR set the task and the tone, but just as culture is what people do when nobody's watching (or at least when the boss isn't watching), how can culture permeate the beliefs and behaviors of every person in an organization? There are several ways, but only one of them is sustainable.

1. The CEO and HR can dedicate every moment of their working lives to promoting company culture.
2. The company can find and hire only people who already completely understand the right culture and will instinctively follow it with no prompting.

3. The company can adopt the practice we call *a culture of recognition*, in which every single employee is responsible for saying "Thanks!"—recognizing, celebrating, appreciating, and promoting the desired cultural values.

We have spent more than a decade studying and crafting a set of practices, beliefs, and values that enable culture to thrive. You might call it an operating system for company culture—an enabling technology for proactive culture management. It is a *culture of recognition*, which is a set of beliefs, habits, and values that affirm and drive all other values, actions, and results of a company.

- Do you want more teamwork?—Then recognize it!
- Do you need innovation?—Then celebrate it!
- Do you want employees to give extra effort (engagement)?—Then acknowledge it!
- Do you believe every expression of a company value is important?—Then appreciate it!

A culture of recognition engages, energizes, and empowers employees; it can mean the difference between failure and success for companies in today's hypercompetitive marketplace. A culture of recognition propels your organization's unique culture ahead. By doing so, it also drives performance and profits.

Senior executives in the C-suite and HR are too busy for Option 1, and Option 2 is almost impossible. That leaves Option 3, and that's what the rest of this book is about.

2 | The People-First Workplace

IHG (InterContinental Hotels Group) has more than 350,000 employees in its owned, managed and franchised hotels, places with familiar names like InterContinental Hotel & Resort, Holiday Inn and Crowne Plaza. To Employer Brand Delivery Manager Ly Bui, social recognition represents a top-to-bottom understanding that delivering the experience of "Great Hotels Guests Love" begins and ends with motivated, engaged and enthusiastic people – what IHG calls "BrandHearted" employees.

"To us, it's about motivating them, making sure that you're taking care of the people who are going to turn around and take care of the guests," says Bui. "Recognized employees see the importance of living our values, and inspire others to do the same. Appreciation is one of the most effective motivators in building long-term employee engagement, and at the end of the day, saying 'Thank you' is just part of showing you care. It's part of being a BrandHearted leader. If we do that, then we have done everything we can."

There's also a personal reward in showing appreciation, Bui says. "I get great pleasure from the unexpected rewards of recognition.

For example, an employee said she and her husband wanted to get a high-definition TV they really couldn't afford. She saved her Bravo awards [IHG's recognition program name] throughout the year. One day she showed me a photo of this big hi-def TV she bought for her family for the holidays using the saved Bravos. She was happy IHG and her peers recognized her, and also happy she was able to use it for her family. They shared in the recognition experience."

*   *   *

The Importance of Empathy

George Anders, a contributing editor at *Forbes*, notes that many of the fastest-growing jobs in the modern economy, from registered nurses to personal finance consultants, require a powerful sense of empathy.[1] Empathy is the ability to put oneself in another's situation. Truly powerful empathy is the ability to understand and anticipate at a deep emotional level someone else's thoughts, feelings, perceptions, pleasures, and displeasures.

Great HR managers we know have an automatic empathy, what psychologist Daniel Goleman called emotional intelligence. But it's not limited to HR managers. Great leaders in product design have an intuitive feel for how people will react to a dress pattern or the feel of a smartphone in the hand. Great leaders in service companies like hospitality and travel do more than merely satisfy customers—they delight them. Great sales professionals seek to understand not only their customers' problems but also how those customers feel about them, because truly sophisticated selling identifies the "right problem to solve," giving the solution the highest perceived value.

Silent empathy won't move a workforce. It must be expressed. People have to learn their leaders and peers understand their work and their effort. The best way to express this is appreciation. At the most basic human level, recognizing effort and saying "thank you" has astonishing power to motivate others.

Appreciation Gives Power to Empathy

William James, one of the founders of modern psychology, wrote in 1896, "The deepest principle of Human Nature is the craving to be appreciated."[2]

A report from payroll processing company ADP illustrates the power of appreciation in the workplace. ADP asked employees and HR directors in Great Britain, "Aside from pay, what motivates and engages you at work?" Fifty-nine percent replied, "Praise and recognition." That was by far the most important motivation after pay—more than employee benefits, clear paths for advancement, or even the flexibility to work where and when the employee wanted.[3]

Why should praise and recognition—receiving thanks—be so motivating? In the context of the modern organization, giving and receiving thanks is a sophisticated form of communication in five ways:

1. *Thanks identify the right behaviors.* Managers identify the right behaviors in advance and as they happen. In any job, the right behaviors expand beyond a list of instructions. Even if someone is doing a carefully prescribed set of actions such as assembling a part on a line or packing products in a warehouse, there are dozens of potential behaviors that have an impact for better or worse. When someone on the shop floor sees an oil spill, he has a choice to clean it, ask someone else to clean it, or say nothing. Each action has consequences, and the right action should be appreciated—first, because it's rewarding to receive thanks, and second, because there will be another oil spill (or other safety hazard) someday soon.

2. *Thanks are feedback. It tells employees they're on the right track.* In complex work environments, actual work results might not appear for some time. Thanks for effort, quickly expressed, reassures employees that they're doing the right things. Even if a project ultimately fails, appreciation reinforces the work that was done right. Without appreciation and instruction, feedback might not be given until the annual performance review.

3. *Thanks break through social and emotional barriers.* Emotional and social barriers are a natural product of hierarchies. Even in the flattest, most egalitarian organizations, someone has ultimate authority, and that power distances the boss from the staff. Sincerely expressed thanks break through the social barriers that naturally arise in organizations. When those barriers fall, emotions like loyalty, trust, and dedication flow more freely.

4. *Thanks create trust and social bonds.* After breaking though social barriers, thanks create social bonds between giver and receiver. Sincerely expressed, thanks also foster trust between employee and manager, and among all employees as peers. In a work environment where trust prevails, "knowledge hoarders" are rare and the transfer of knowledge between individuals and teams is far more common.

5. *Thanks feel good.* This is obvious! Yet ask a manager if it's her job to make others feel good, and the questions start coming—feel good about what? We argue that feeling good is a benefit of appreciation but only has strategic value if it reinforces the right behaviors. It's nice to be thanked for your lovely singing voice, but the appreciation that counts in a business is being recognized for your amazing dedication to customer satisfaction.

Expert Insight

"We don't want to recognize someone just for coming in on the weekend or working late. While admirable, those extra hours are not beneficial if not spent on working on the right projects or arriving at the results needed. We focus on recognizing both the 'how' (behaviors and values) as well as the 'what' (the results)."

—Rob Schmitter, BlackBerry

Assume that managers have empathy and know how to express appreciation. Why doesn't it happen more often? Leigh Branham, author of *The 7 Hidden Reasons Employees Leave*, studied more than

100,000 verbatim responses in various best-employer surveys and identified 13 reasons managers fall short when it comes to recognizing their people. Some reasons will be familiar to most HR directors: lack of time, lack of attention to employee performance, fears that appreciation will seem unnecessary or insincere. Other reasons indicate basic management flaws such as disrespect for workers and lack of understanding of their employees' jobs. The underlying theme of Branham's 13 reasons is this: Managers misunderstand the psychology and mechanics of recognition. They assume employees are motivated by the most basic rewards and punishments, and they fail to see the workplace as a dynamic social system. Giving thanks and appreciation isn't habitual for these managers because it hasn't been taught as a management discipline in a complex work environment.[4]

Steve Kerr, former chief learning officer at General Electric and Goldman Sachs, pointed out a seeming paradox in his excellent book *Reward Systems*. In addition to compensation, Kerr observed the value of "content rewards." These are interactions with others, such as feedback from managers and recognition. He then observed, "Ironically because we're so attached to the idea that value comes from scarcity . . . the unlimited availability [of content rewards] may be why so many managers underutilize them. Never underestimate the power of metrics to signal that something is important."[5]

As the presence of metrics signals that something is important, a lack of metrics has the opposite effect. The key to creating more recognition and manager feedback is not to insist it's different from all other management disciplines but to treat it just like all other management disciplines—and measure it. (We'll show you how in Chapters 5, 7, and 8.)

Would You Withhold Praise from Your Children?

Think about children in your life, whether your own or others whom you love and interact with often. How many times a day do you praise them or express your love for them: three or five or twenty times?

Now imagine this: One day you decide it's just too much work to constantly praise and love your children. It's just too time consuming to constantly pay attention to what they're doing well or things they are learning and praise them for it. So you decide, instead of the daily effort, you'll store all that goodwill, affection and positivity up for the child's birthday. Then, on their special day, you'll make an extra effort with an over-the-top birthday extravaganza, complete with bounce houses, entertainment, maybe even a pony!

Would you feel that scenario was better for your child than hearing words of praise and love several times a day? Of course not! (Indeed, recent research shows such neglect shrinks important parts of the developing brain, causing many unintended consequences.)[6] We want our children to know when they're doing well and how much we support them as they learn and grow.

Of course, our work colleagues are not our children, yet we think we can make people valued by recognizing them one day a year, and ignoring them the other 364 days.

Giving praise at work is the same as giving praise at home—many small repetitions and sincere expressions of thanks and positivity are much more powerful than one big annual "appreciation."

Happiness at Work

Eric's book *The Crowdsourced Performance Review* summarized social science research about the importance of happiness at work. Positive emotions, feelings of fulfillment, well-being, and optimism, have been proven through decades of experimentation to boost creative problem solving.[7] In a modern workplace, that creative problem solving is the heart of continuous improvement, innovation, process management, and the other factors that constitute knowledge work. That feeds the positive cycle of emotions and behaviors that we saw in Chapter 1 (values → behaviors → emotions → change), which leads an employee to become more energized and engaged. As we've seen, an energized and engaged workforce produces better financial results.[8]

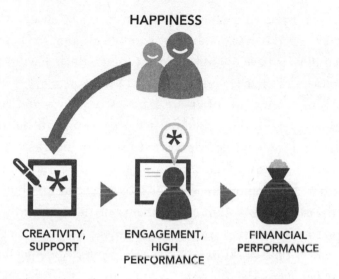

HAPPINESS

CREATIVITY,
SUPPORT

ENGAGEMENT,
HIGH
PERFORMANCE

FINANCIAL
PERFORMANCE

Figure 2.1 The path to financial performance begins with workplace happiness

An illustration from Eric's book summarizes the connection (Figure 2.1).

Happiness at work is a financial imperative because it leads directly to higher performance. Lest anyone confuse happiness with simple pleasure or wish fulfillment, let's look at it a little closer in the context of work.

For each individual, happiness at work is the product of many factors working together, which range from the most basic factors such as physical safety and adequate pay to more subjective, "higher," factors such as workplace relationships and a sense that work is something more than just a way to make a living.

The employer controls the basic factors and can encourage (but not fully control) the higher factors, for example by hiring people who are clearly aligned with a company's mission and values. (Tony Hsieh, founder and CEO of online retailer Zappos.com and author of *Delivering Happiness*, embodies this principle to the extent that Zappos will pay people to quit if, after a period of work, they don't agree with the company's mission.[9] Recently, Zappos's parent company, Amazon, announced it would follow Zappos's lead.)

How can an employer encourage those higher factors that lead to happiness at work? The same way managers achieve anything through other people: by setting expectations, directing actions, and communicating expected behaviors. It's not enough to hope for happiness at work—employers have to model and encourage the behaviors that lead to happiness, and these are primarily social behaviors.

Study any annual list of an area's best workplaces and you'll find similarities—great working conditions, fair pay, work-life balance—and you'll also find frequent descriptions of those intangible social factors such as support, a sense of mission, encouragement, optimism, and teamwork. In-demand employers encourage those social factors, but they only exist to the extent the workforce acts them out, day after day. The vision and inspiration might start with the CEO (indeed, it must), but it thrives because most of the workforce participates in the vision long term.

These behaviors, demonstrated voluntarily week after week, in every corner of a healthy company, create what we call a *Positivity Dominated Workplace*, where everyone is invested in promoting a culture of engagement, energy, risk-taking, risk-management, candor, caring, and any other combination of behaviors that constitute the company's culture.

"When You're Happier, You're Smarter"

When Captain David Marquet was appointed skipper of the nuclear submarine *Santa Fe*, it was considered the worst boat in the undersea service. It had poor evaluation scores, and morale was so bad that prior to his command, only three sailors out of 135 had reenlisted.

With only weeks to turn around the situation, Marquet reversed his academy-learned concept of leader-follower management (in which the leader gives all commands and everyone follows) in favor of a model he called leader-leader. Officers and enlisted sailors were told to think for themselves, without waiting for orders on such mundane tasks as acquiring parts for a worn-out pump. Marquet broke down "silo" thinking with the slogan "There's no *they* on *Santa Fe*." Nobody was allowed to assume, "They'll do it" or "It's their fault."

Instead, he instructed, everyone was to think and behave like a leader, to take the initiative and work together. Marquet's goal was to raise morale by giving control to sailors who felt they had no control. Without condescension, he says he wanted to see what would happen to performance if sailors were happy in their work.

Within weeks *Santa Fe* earned dramatically better scores in evaluations by senior naval officers. Within two years, it was rated first in the service. After Marquet left command, the boat was still earning stellar scores and promoting its crew, including 10 subsequent submarine captains.

Marquet realized his received wisdom—if you improve performance, morale will improve—was wrong. In fact, the opposite was a more effective management model. When he treated his crew as if they were capable of thinking for themselves, making the right decisions, and reinforcing each other's good work—which boosted morale immediately—better results followed. Marquet has since become a leadership consultant, Columbia University teacher, author, and speaker who observes, "When you're happier, you don't just act smarter, you actually *are* smarter."[10]

The Positivity Dominated Workplace

Positivity is the conviction that "it's up to me to make things turn out all right." Positivity looks at a business win and says, "We did this," and looks at a business loss and says, "We can turn this reversal into a chance to get better." Positivity embraces challenge and even setbacks with a sense of efficacy. It's not only about good times; it's about taking personal responsibility for good times and bad.

In the Positivity Dominated Workplace, employees and managers are encouraging each other, learning from successes and failures, noticing and celebrating and, above all, recognizing the behaviors that embody company values and advance company goals.

Those two words—*recognizing* and *behaviors*—are the foundation of a Positivity Dominated Workplace. Recognition matters because it reinforces the right actions, encouraging them to happen again and again, providing guidance, and adding social value. Behaviors matter because in a workplace, behavior trumps intention. Behavior, not intentions or even ideas, makes profits and achieves missions. The Positivity Dominated Workplace is first and last an active, achievement-oriented institution.

A Positivity Dominated Workplace might be a manufacturer, a high-tech devices company, a design firm, a religious institution, or a global hotel chain. Positivity is agnostic when it comes to whether a workforce is filled with MBAs or short-haul truckers or bakers or accountants. Most big companies have a wide range of skills and jobs; positivity does not discriminate about the kind of work being done but focuses on how it is being done, how people feel about their work and their role and their value. Engagement flows from people doing work they like well in a culture that appreciates and recognizes a job well done.

Authenticity and Transparency

Two additional factors characterize the people-first workplace, from the mightiest global brands to the most successful small businesses. They are *authenticity* and *transparency*.

Authenticity means people are living the same company culture that the CEO describes and that the HR department claims in job descriptions. Nike employees really care about winning. Apple people really do worry about the tiniest invisible details of a product. GE executives and line workers alike strive for Six Sigma consistency in products and processes. The counter help at a Wegmans supermarket deli behave as if slicing a pound of Swiss cheese the way you like it is the most important thing they will do that day.

Employees have a built-in authenticity detector, and the executive whose speech about company mission is met with silence or eye rolling has triggered the alarm. He or she may pay or pressure people into compliance, but the vision will not sustain itself. Employees must believe in the mission to truly support it, and the only path to that belief is authenticity.

Transparency is a relatively new quality of the workplace, accelerated by the Internet in general and social media in particular. In the past, a company could promote a false image of itself in the media (or job advertisements) as an exciting and rewarding place to work with no easy way for an applicant to check. Now a current or prospective employee can go on a dozen social media sites from Facebook to Glassdoor to read what employees say about a workplace. This can even have entertainment value: in September 2013 a video producer posted a dancing "I Quit!" video critical of her employer on YouTube. It got millions of views, so much so that the employer responded with a video showing happy employees also singing and dancing (with the final message, "by the way . . . we're hiring").[11] This kind of transparency was unthinkable before YouTube and the millennial habit of speaking out to the world.

For a company striving to build a great workplace, a great employer brand, and a fully engaged, productive workforce, there is no longer a choice. Because the reality of a workplace is now public information, and a company's culture of whatever stripe must be authentic, the necessary task is to motivate people to celebrate and promote that authentic culture.

As Captain Marquet learned, that means focusing on the things that create happiness and high morale so that a Positivity Dominated Workplace can grow and thrive.

That begins with understanding the power of giving and receiving appreciation, the subject of Chapter 3.

3 Appreciation, Gratitude, and Employee Engagement

Intuit, the maker of personal and business finance software, is known for combining innovation with simplicity in its products, and in recent years it has focused heavily on mobile technologies. But Intuit is also known as a best place to work because of its people-centric culture.

Intuit's popular recognition program (called Spotlight) works in ways congruent with Intuit's tech-savvy, cutting-edge values. The recognition program is tightly tied to how Intuit measures and preserves its exceptional employee engagement scores. You'd expect a company like Intuit to manage an enterprise-wide recognition program scientifically. But what's really powerful is how the company embraces the emotions released, and meaningful human connections made, when people recognize each other.

In a recent survey more than 90 percent of award recipients said that receiving recognition helps them to continue to deliver above-and-beyond results. Employees say they love the positive feedback they get from their managers and each other.

Recognition at Intuit is social in the best sense, according to the survey. Employees say they share their recognition experience with their colleagues, friends, and family. Intuit's goodwill thus influences a much broader audience than just the recipients of awards.

*   *   *

While happiness at work makes people smarter, more engaged, and more productive, people also have a similar but distinct need to achieve a sense of meaning in what they do.[1] Happiness is about the self; feelings of meaning at work arise from the social context.

The feeling that what you do has meaning beyond your own gratification is cultural. It is confirmed by satisfying a cultural set of values (as when one feels attached to a religion, a nation, or a set of associates).[2] In a society, it's noticed and confirmed by others. Meaning is associated with giving more than taking, with contributing to something bigger than oneself.

Assuming that it's good for employees to find meaning in their work, how can employers encourage that? What reinforces an employee's sense of belonging to something greater than him- or herself?

The answer is found in the social behavior of *expressing appreciation and gratitude*. The two go hand in hand: Appreciation means recognizing work well done. It is a subjective expression in the same way one "appreciates" a work of art or a clever solution to a work problem. When I express appreciation for your work, I might simply be noticing its quality or benefit. I might be having a good day and want to share my sense of satisfaction and belonging.

Gratitude is a bit more personal than appreciation—it means expressing thanks for a benefit one has received. When I express gratitude to you for a job well done, it's because I have received direct or indirect value. If I'm your manager, I might express gratitude for you going beyond expectations and making the group more productive, which advances my own goals. If I'm your peer, I might be grateful because you stopped by to help me fix a problem even though you could have ignored it (and me).

Appreciation and gratitude are powerful forces among employees because they satisfy the higher psychological needs of individuals and the higher social needs of groups. They confer meaning on actions because they show an action is either recognized as valuable (appreciated) or personally beneficial (gratitude) or both.

This is a big deal in managing because it makes the workplace a source of meaning. To understand the potential power of appreciation and gratitude, consider human needs from the most basic to the most sophisticated.

A Hierarchy of Human Needs[3]

Psychologist Abraham Maslow's classic hierarchy of human needs (see Figure 3.1) is a model for considering the importance of gratitude in work and in life. The most basic needs are related to physical survival. The next most important are the needs for a sense of safety, social contact, self-esteem, recognition, and status. The highest need (and psychological achievement) is called self-actualization.

Maslow's pyramid can be seen as a metaphor for what a workplace can potentially provide, from the pay that ensures food and shelter, to safety and social contact, to self-esteem. Self-actualization in the organization can be seen in those who love their work, who find their identity and satisfaction from their work, and who are "a perfect fit" with the organization.

The higher you climb in Maslow's hierarchy, the more individualized the needs become. Physical needs are pretty much the same no matter

Figure 3.1 Maslow's hierarchy of human needs

who the person is—everyone needs food and water. Safety needs are more individual, but there are plenty of guidelines for creating a physically and psychologically safe workplace. Social needs require a workplace that functions socially, in which company culture encourages socially productive interactions. Esteem needs and self-actualization are uniquely shaped from the perspective of each person.

Appreciation and Employee Needs

Maslow's hierarchy of human needs has much to teach about the power of appreciation. The highest needs—social, esteem, and self-actualization— are all fed and nurtured by appreciation.

The mediocre manager likes to think that his or her employees should be grateful to have a job. Perhaps they are, but that attitude has culture management backward. In a well-run company, the organization and the individual manager acting on its behalf harness the power of appreciation not by receiving it, but by giving it to the employees.

Let's look at the aspects of appreciation that make it essential to culture management:

Thanks are motivating. People like being thanked. It feels good to affirm employees' worth and value. How do they get more thanks? By repeating the behavior that wins the thanks.

Thanks are humanizing. The ability to express appreciation is a key strength in a leader. Appreciation is an emotion that, in many cultures, actually lends power to someone else, in the expectation that he or she will receive it. Can you imagine having your thanks rejected? It makes the person saying "thank you" a little less exalted, a little more human.

Thanks are specific. "Thank you" is reacting to a specific act, achievement, or attitude that's recognized in the transaction. It also lends credence to the importance and value of that act.

Thanks are empowering. First, appreciation empowers by affirming the power of the individual to make a choice. (I don't have to earn your appreciation, but I choose to.) Second, because appreciation can be expressed by anyone in the hierarchy to anyone else in the hierarchy, it is a reward that potentially cuts across the class and culture lines of an organization.

Thanks are powerful. Spiritual leaders emphasize the importance of gratitude on the path to wholeness. National leaders thank soldiers for their service; mayors offer the thanks of a grateful public to first responders to emergency situations. And notice how often the most enlightened business leaders attribute their success openly and often to their employees. Appreciation establishes a psychological contract between employees. Complete that contract, and you are assured of more productive relations among workers. Break that contract, and you are assured of higher turnover, lower engagement, and a population of employees who deliver below their full potential.

Research Insight

Seventy-one percent of Millennials reported meaningful work was among the three most important factors defining career success, while 30 percent believed it was the most critical factor.[4]

Wharton professor Adam Grant, author of *Give and Take*, believes that appreciation goes a long way to connect people in an organization. In a recent interview he told us, "When recognition rises in an organization, that can be a binding and connecting force. It elicits a lot of positive emotion, because people tend to enjoy both expressing and receiving gratitude. The effect can also travel in the reverse. When you have stronger emotional connections, you tend to be more appreciative. There can be a virtuous cycle."[5]

Gratitude Spreads Value Around

As appreciation builds a healthy culture, gratitude promotes a healthy workforce (and not just in terms of physical health).

It's tempting to underestimate this simple truth about human beings: giving thanks benefits both giver and receiver. Gratitude magnifies the spirit and promotes well-being. In good times and bad, authentic appreciation creates perspective, literally stepping back from the distractions of the moment and affirming something more lasting than passing circumstance.

This is more than proverb or opinion. Serious scientific research on the effects of gratitude has taken place globally for at least two decades. Here are 14 beneficial effects of gratitude on the health of individuals and their workplaces:[6]

1. *Grateful people achieve more.* Studies show gratitude promotes significant increases in determination, attention, enthusiasm and energy, academic attainment, and even athletic achievement.
2. *Grateful people are better corporate citizens.* Studies of corporate employees demonstrate a positive relationship between gratitude and corporate social responsibility. One study's authors said, "Employees with stronger hope and gratitude were found to have a greater sense of responsibility toward employee and societal issues."
3. *Grateful people are less likely to burn out.* A 2010 study found an inverse relationship between dispositional gratitude and workplace burnout in teachers in China. Additional research found that when patients and managers provided gratitude and recognition to employees who worked in career roles for HIV/AIDS patients, it buffered those employees from burnout.
4. *Grateful people pay it forward.* A 2006 study at Northwestern University found subjects who had been helped with a task were more likely to volunteer to help someone else with an unrelated, time-intensive task. Research has also found that expressing thanks doubles the likelihood that a benefactor will repeat the behavior for which one is grateful.[7]
5. *Grateful people are more morally alert.* Gratitude is used as a "moral motive" in that it encourages social behavior and discourages disruptive behavior. A workplace is a small society that benefits in both tangible and intangible ways from people behaving morally.
6. *Giving creates a positive feedback loop.* A 2009 Harvard Business School study found: "Happier people give more and giving makes

people happier, such that happiness and giving may operate in a positive feedback loop (with happier people giving more, getting happier, and giving even more)."

7. *Opportunity to give increases commitment to a company.* Wharton School professor Adam Grant studied a Fortune 500 company that allowed employees to contribute to an employee beneficiary fund. He found donors rather than beneficiaries had the greater increase in their affective commitment to the company.

8. *Givers are more engaged.* The Summer 2013 Globoforce Workforce Mood Tracker study found employees who had been empowered to give recognition to peers were more than twice as engaged as those who were not.

9. *Gratefulness increases emotional well-being.* Gratitude improves individual well-being independent of personality. Over time, gratitude leads to lower stress and depression and higher levels of social support.

10. *Grateful people get along better with others.* People who express gratitude are more extroverted, agreeable, open, and conscientious as well as less neurotic.

11. *Grateful people are more resilient to trauma.* Gratitude is significant in helping people maintain emotional well-being after traumatic life experiences.

12. *Grateful people sleep better.* Several studies have found that higher levels of gratitude were associated with better sleep (and recent sleep studies are increasing awareness of its importance in a host of benefits from energy to optimism).

13. *Grateful people are physically healthier.* Gratitude strengthens the immune system, lowers blood pressure, reduces symptoms of illness, increases resistance to pain, correlates with better exercise habits, and encourages us to take better care of our health.

14. *Grateful people are less depressed.* Researchers from three major universities found that study participants who wrote and delivered a letter of gratitude to someone who had been kind to them, but never properly thanked, showed a boost in happiness and a decrease in depression. They called on therapists to employ gratitude as a clinical tool.

Psychic Income

Human beings have a fundamental need for social acceptance, increased self-esteem, and self-realization.[8] In a business setting, these needs can never be met by cash compensation, which organizational psychologist Frederick Herzberg found could only prevent people from being dissatisfied.[9] Salary is what we call tangible income—vitally important, but directly related to material needs as well as status or power. Study after study shows that nonmonetary rewards are the key to improved performance. These rewards, which we call *psychic income*, are cost-effective as well. They are more flexible, affordable, and immediate than salary.

Psychic income is the provision of social acceptance, social esteem (leading to self-esteem), and self-actualization. Paid in the "currency" of recognition, psychic income is intangible but no less real than material income. And you don't have to wait until payday to make a deposit.

This is reminiscent of leadership guru Stephen R. Covey's metaphor of the "Emotional Bank Account."[10] Covey's model portrays acts like courtesy, respect, and honesty as deposits in the account, and discourtesy, disrespect, and dishonesty as withdrawals. The balance in Covey's Emotional Bank Account is the amount of trust in a relationship.

Research Insight

More than half (53 percent) of those surveyed say their boss is dishonest, and the same amount say their boss is unfair, according to a survey by the Adecco Group. Others described bosses as impatient (58 percent), disloyal (66 percent), and lacking motivational skills (76 percent). These numbers are staggering, given that nearly all (89 percent) say that the employee/boss relationship is one of the most important links to job satisfaction.[11]

So it is with psychic income. Managers and executives pay out psychic income to employees with acts of respect, esteem, dignity, and high regard. They reduce psychic income with acts of disrespect, humiliation, disinterest, and low regard. The balance between these is the amount of psychic wealth accumulated at work.

Another powerful metaphor, created by Gallup researcher Donald O. Clifton and his collaborator Tom Rath, is the theory they called "The Dipper and the Bucket." Everyone has a psychological "bucket" that is emptied or filled constantly, depending on what others say or do to us. A full bucket is positive, an empty bucket negative, depending on all the factors we've discussed. Everyone also has a psychological "dipper" that works in the opposite way from the real thing: when we use our dipper to fill other people's buckets, by saying or doing things that increase their positive emotions, our own buckets are filled as well. And when we use that metaphorical dipper to take away from others' buckets by saying or doing things that cause negative emotions, our own buckets likewise are diminished. The seeming paradox cited by Clifton and Rath (as well as positivity psychologists) is that the more positivity we provide, the more positivity we acquire.[12]

The impact gets really interesting when psychic income is paid by managers. When McKinsey compared the motivating power of cash versus noncash rewards, it found the "top three nonfinancial motivators [praise from immediate managers, leadership attention . . . and a chance to lead projects or task forces] play critical roles in making employees feel their companies value them, take their well-being seriously, and strive to create opportunities for career growth." The survey states these three noncash motivators are more effective than cash.[13]

The Power of Positive Reinforcement

Even in tough-minded cultures, positive reinforcement is a powerful driver of culture. U.S. Marine training might be strenuous and even abusive, but that initiation process is not the culture. The stress of Marine boot camp serves as much to *identify*

Marines as to train them. Once established as a Marine, a recruit experiences profound recognition on a daily basis—reinforced by the mottos, the uniform, the unit cohesion, the intense group loyalty. Marines display recognition for their service and sacrifice on their uniforms in the form of medals, ribbons, and rank insignia. All these inspire pride and internal reward. Marine culture is intensely about recognition. Listen to retired Marines in conversation—twenty years after their service ended, they'll still call each other "Marine," and mean it as a badge of honor.

Harvard Business School Professor Teresa Amabile and her collaborator Steven Kramer conducted a rigorous analysis of employee motivation, presenting their results in *The Progress Principle*. They wrote, "We found that the most important indicator on employee engagement . . . was simply 'making progress in meaningful work.' If employees could find meaning to the work—even contributing value to the team or the organization—this would make a difference."[14] Furthermore, a satisfying "inner work life," which is key to progress, is fed by four factors they called Nourishers: respect, encouragement, emotional support (especially in the form of empathy from a manager), and affiliation.

The four factors are metaphorical deposits in Covey's emotional bank account or Clifton and Rath's bucket. To the extent that managers (and peers) give respect, recognition, encouragement, emotional support, and affiliation, they are making deposits of goodwill and energy in each other's lives . . . and that capital can be spent in productive activities.

It's entirely the employee's choice whether she or he spends that capital by directing energy into productive activities, aligned to the company strategy and affirming company values. Managers encourage that choice with timely, specific recognition and appreciation of progress (making it real) and by calling out the importance of even incremental progress to the larger goal (making it meaningful).

Employee Engagement

If you're reading this book, you want engaged employees. Engagement is the HR hot topic of the decade.

First, a definition: Engagement at work is the willingness to give discretionary effort to a job. It means voluntarily doing more than the minimum. It is an attitude confirmed by behavior. An engaged employee is aligned to strategy and committed to delivering on his or her goals as well as the strategic goals of the company. The connection between engagement and higher performance is obvious and is well established in nationwide and global studies.

Engagement at work is rare, however, and that lack of engagement costs hundreds of billions. Gallup's "State of the American Workplace" report from June 2013 reported the baleful effect of the *non*engaged workforce:

"The vast majority of U.S. workers, 70%, are 'not engaged' or 'actively disengaged' at work, meaning they are emotionally disconnected from their workplace and are less likely to be productive. Actively disengaged employees alone cost the U.S. between $450 billion to $550 billion each year in lost productivity, and are more likely than engaged employees to steal from their companies, negatively influence their coworkers, miss workdays, and drive customers away."

Expert Insight

"One of the wonderful things about the recognition program we call Bravo is that it has been able to provide us with data. Data any time that we need to be able to see top performers, top performing teams and the reasons why. Our employee engagement survey is an emotional survey because it asks about how happy, motivated, proud an employee is to come to work. The Bravo recognition program is probably the only set of data I have to be able to reinforce that engagement level. It's been great to see employees recognizing each other and managers recognizing their direct reports."

—Ly Bui, Employer Brand Delivery
Manager, IHG

The HR consultancy Towers Watson found similar results in its 2002 Global Workforce Study, establishing that only 35 percent of global employees were "highly engaged" at work.[15]

Engaged employees are important contributors to the company's culture and continually reinforce values that support the company mission as well as the bottom line. At its most powerful, recognition continuously propagates and reinforces desired behaviors throughout the company.

What happens to the disengaged employee? The number-one reason people leave their current employer is the feeling they don't count, that their work was not recognized. "I wasn't valued. My contributions weren't appreciated," is the common explanation. This leads to disaffection and alienation—the psychic opposite of engagement.

Towers Watson suggests that the way to sustain engagement is to see that a workforce is *enabled* (has an environment that supports productivity and performance with the right equipment, knowledge, help, and other resources) and *energized* (has a sense of individual, physical, interpersonal, and emotional well-being at work.)[16]

MYTHBUSTER
"If you want to get something done, give it to a busy person."

One of the ways that employees may be recognized for their good work on a project is to be given another important, intense project. As the saying goes, "The reward for solving a problem is getting another problem."

Something's missing in that scenario. Before rewarding a successful person with more hard work, take a moment to acknowledge that the work he or she has completed was great. Rather than imply the statement, "Clearly I trust you to do good work. Isn't that enough recognition for you?" People actually want to hear, "Thank you, that was an outstanding performance!"

Assigning tough projects helps make successful careers, but don't miss out on the simple human connection as well.

Enablement, Energy, Empowerment, Encouragement

Enablement is a subjective experience because the employee sees himself in a context. For example: Say I'm an auditor and I want a desktop calculator because I work better that way. I can tap out accurate calculations without having to look at the specialized keyboard. My boss says, "You have a calculator on the computer, just use that." But that's not how I work best—I have to tap out the numbers along the top of my large computer keyboard. That might only make a few seconds of difference in efficiency and occasional inaccuracy, but it makes a big difference in my comfort and sense of efficacy. Furthermore, the boss has just told me that an inexpensive improvement to my productivity isn't worthwhile. What does that say about my value?

Energy is also a subjective experience affected by work context. Say I'm that auditor and for a week I've been working until 8:00 p.m. every night, closing out the quarterly audit. I'm tired, I've missed time with my family, but I found the energy to do it because I'm dedicated to the task. If nobody appreciates that extra effort, I've paid out a lot of extra energy with no extra payback. I've given a lot more than I have to, but received the same as last week (a paycheck).

If instead my boss expresses gratitude for my extra effort, my whole social context changes for the better, especially if that expression is public within the company. The workplace affirms my extra work was valuable, worthwhile, and appreciated. (And if the boss accompanies that expression with a tangible reward, that effect is magnified.)

Writing in the *Harvard Business Review*, Tony Schwartz and Catherine McCarthy note that when organizations demand higher performance from their employees, those workers typically put in more hours at work. Schwartz and McCarthy say this is the wrong focus. Instead, the authors recommend that companies support a focus on managing each employee's physical, emotional, and spiritual energy. Their case studies show employees who manage energy well demonstrate significant improvements in performance.[17]

We believe *empowerment* and *encouragement* are additional factors that nurture and sustain engagement over the long run.

Empowerment transfers the power to achieve results from the manager to the employee. Once enabled with the right resources, an employee must be empowered to take responsibility, to make decisions, and to act with those resources. Empowerment is the foundation of accountability—that is, delivering on commitments. Engaged and productive employees are by definition empowered to achieve results.

> *Engaged and productive employees are by definition empowered to achieve results.*

Encouragement is another of those human factors that go far in making an engaged workforce. At its simplest, encouragement costs practically nothing—a word, a bit of recognition, a gesture of appreciation or gratitude—yet it literally "gives courage" to an employee to act again, to go beyond the minimum, to break out of the sterile job requirements, to take risks, and to make the extra effort that defines engagement in the first place.

Thanks, appreciation, gratitude, recognition, well-being, and engagement are qualities of a healthy and well-functioning workplace. Every business leader can want the results that derive from these competitive advantages over lesser workplaces, but not every business leader succeeds in creating them. In Part 2, we'll show how a company's social architecture can be designed to deliver on their promise.

PART 2
UNDERSTANDING SOCIAL RECOGNITION

4 | Setting a Purpose and a Vision

Baker Hughes is a $22 billion provider of technology and services to develop oil fields. Most of their 60,000 employees don't sit in offices at computers, says Ryan Hill, the director of total rewards, global and executive compensation. "They're on ships, on drilling platforms in the Gulf of Mexico, in the remote plains of North Dakota. They're working in West Texas and talking on a cell phone to someone in Louisiana or Dubai." Employees work in 70-plus countries around the globe.

Growing recognition in such a disparate and decentralized company begins with setting a vision: What will recognition achieve? How can it reinforce company values? How will recognition work in harmony with the ways people already communicate and work together?

"Ultimately, our ambition is for people to feel a part of the organization, so they want to stay and contribute," says Hill. "We decided to focus on employee engagement and retention [which means] we have a highly motivated workforce that enjoys working at Baker Hughes and contributing to the success of the company."

Hill had a simple, observable operational goal as well. He wanted to change the cadence of recognition from a typical years-of-service award, which happened infrequently. Now, he says, "When managers really interact with their employees on an ongoing basis, and recognize the things close to when they're done, we know we have an effective program."

*   *   *

One of the most widely misunderstood quotations in business is Louis V. Gerstner's July 1993 statement, "The last thing IBM needs right now is a vision." Gerstner, an outsider brought in as CEO to rescue the tottering computer giant, was not saying a vision is inherently bad; he was emphasizing that IBM's first step to recovery was getting its operations in order, cutting costs, and discarding unprofitable activities. Just seven months later, in fact, Gerstner's annual message to IBM shareholders described the sea change in IBM's business and culture with the agnostic statement: "Some call it mission. Some call it vision. I call it strategy."[1]

Whatever it was called, it worked. IBM's historic recovery, based on offering customers "solutions" instead of products, remade the company and reoriented strategic thinking for a generation of executives. In his book about the turnaround, *Who Says Elephants Can't Dance?*, Gerstner emphasizes the centrality of changing IBM's culture, not only with a mission or vision statement but also by demanding changes in behavior (such as ending competition between divisions) and making decisions that nobody stuck in the old culture would have dared make (such as conceding the operating system war to Microsoft). Gerstner tied employee compensation to "personal business commitments," which were individual rather than divisional results. While his first changes were operational, his long-term changes were cultural.[2]

As an outsider, Gerstner was well positioned to describe a new purpose and vision, but he needed IBM's employees to achieve them. Some employees, chastened by the company's near-death experience, were willing and able to change. Others left voluntarily, opening IBM to new employees who could adopt a new culture.

Over a decade, IBM's cultural changes, played out in daily actions by each employee, took it from survival to resurgence.

Culture and the Heroic Leader

Worldwide, organizations revere the heroic leader—the man or woman whose vision and willpower create (and enforce) a particular culture. This celebration parallels the fascination with celebrity itself: *People* and other magazines revel in fame even as they create it. Business media picked up this trend with endless stories about cultural leaders like Gerstner, Richard Branson of Virgin, Alan Mulally of Ford, Bill Gates of Microsoft, and Steve Jobs of Apple. Each had definite visions of his company's culture. Each was the antithesis of the boring or nearly anonymous corporate leadership at other companies in their industries as well as the "organization men" of the 1950s and 1960s. And each made a compelling and colorful figure.

Lesser leaders bought into the implied notion that one person creates a unique and successful organizational culture. They tried to imitate the heroic leader's position as the one indispensable person around whose vision all activity took place. The imitators rarely succeeded because they credited the individual and his vision alone. They failed to see that cultural change only becomes permanent when most of a company's employees embrace the change and live it out through the workaday world. Even if they accomplished "the vision thing," the imitators' efforts broke down in the all-important implementation of that vision over days and years.

It's no wonder: getting everyone to embrace a new company culture is no small matter. Alan Murray, deputy managing editor of the *Wall Street Journal*, observed, "As a manager, you may have the power to change your organization's policies with the stroke of a pen. . . . But changing an entrenched culture is the toughest task you will face."[3]

Compounding the problem of change is the daunting task of effectively communicating any culture at all. In 2012, Gallup found only 41 percent of employees felt they knew what their company stands for![4]

Many CEOs hope the senior team will extend culture by passing on what the boss says, or translating the boss's values into their individual styles as they manage their departments. Soon, multiple executives are working within their own spheres of influence, and the cultural norms and imperatives the CEO feels are important become diluted further. Managers pursue different business drivers, different imperatives, different problems and opportunities. Social hierarchies complicate the picture: If the company has a go-go sales culture, then the sales representatives are the royalty. If it's a product culture, the product managers are the princes and princesses of the realm. Different "tribes" tend to believe their culture is best, whatever the CEO urges.

In the business classic *Good to Great: Why Some Companies Make the Leap . . . and Others Don't*, Jim Collins describes the "level 5 leader" as a frequently colorless public figure, yet one focused on many of the social mechanisms of an organization. His analysis shows the drawbacks of a heroic leader, including the obvious fact that an organization dependent on one person for its success gets in trouble when that person leaves, retires, or dies. Great leaders, says Collins, live more often out of the public view but build behavior-based values like "facing the bad news" and a "culture of discipline" into their organizations' DNA.

Many charismatic leaders occupy a central place in the spectrum, well known and inspiring in their industries yet not assuming (or courting) heroic status. Entrepreneurs such as Dr. Amar Bose, founder of Bose Corporation, built cultures that live on after their retirements or deaths. As Bose's name became synonymous with excellence in acoustical engineering (designing high-end music systems and headphones), he worked to create a culture of innovation and broad inquiry. Obituaries at his death in 2013 noted the MIT course he taught was as much about philosophy and personal behavior as it was about acoustical engineering.[5]

Great leaders set a purpose and vision for a company by the goals they establish, the values they promote, and the destination they describe. Then they empower the organization to build culture itself, guided by their vision. They hire people who will promote and demonstrate the right cultural values. They build and promote a *social architecture* that supports the culture they want.

MYTHBUSTER
The Chief Culture Officer

"We need a Chief Culture Officer!" says the CEO, and the search is on to find someone who will spread the word about recognition, and talk about the culture, and arrange events and programs that promote the values. . . .

Wait. There already *is* a Chief Culture Officer, and it's the person the CEO sees in the mirror. If culture is that important—and it is—then the CEO has to promote it relentlessly. Otherwise it's a "nice to have."

Social Architecture

Social architecture is to culture what a foundation, beams, and joists are to a building. Social architecture is found in a thousand small behaviors: communication, traditions, authority, privileges, and "ways of doing things."

It takes a value like "determination" and translates it into situational behaviors like "No matter what, we will never give up on a sale." It is the framework of communication, positive and negative reinforcement, public and private knowledge, and cultural cues that determine how the company will operate. It includes behavior cues like how people dress, how they talk to one another, and even the manners and traditions of the company. It includes how excellence is recognized and rewarded.

Social architecture is useful because no manager can be everywhere, on every phone call, standing beside every employee whenever they're doing anything. It's the set of behavioral norms that define a culture—"what you do when nobody is looking."

> *Social architecture is to culture what a foundation,
> beams, and joists are to a building.*

Jack Welch led GE through enormous changes—the Work Out program for breaking down bureaucracy and Six Sigma processes are just two he oversaw—and his vision, uncompromising standards, and astute use of media aided his success. GE was and is a vast, worldwide organization with hundreds of thousands of employees in scores of countries. He couldn't meet with every employee to persuade them to perform to his standards in his way. He needed a methodology and a structure that would nurture the values he deemed most important. He needed employees to act according to GE values even when nobody was looking. So he posited a set of principles that defined how work would be measured, evaluated, and judged, and he embedded a set of behaviors into GE's social architecture.

GE's managers were evaluated on how thoroughly they applied Welch's principles to their divisions and departments. GE had been a social entity and a successful company for 100 years before Welch took the reins; that social architecture was available to Welch to drive his initiatives throughout the organization. Adapting along the way, he improved communication and impressed every employee with his determination to fight for his values. To cite one example, Welch's dictum to fire the bottom 10 percent based on objective performance criteria promoted hardheaded management and fairness simultaneously. The rating and shedding of poor performers yearly became part of GE's social architecture, one that promoted achievement and a sense of being the best. It certainly had a cost in company image, but it was consistent with the culture Welch intended.

Welch's less skilled imitators confused his cultural *message* of building a winning team with the *method* of getting rid of the bottom 10 percent, leading to culture-killing practices like "stack ranking" in performance reviews.[6] Without the cultural context of GE, in which winning was a primary value reinforced in a hundred additional ways, the practice only sowed mistrust and gamesmanship.

Executive Insight

"The middle 70 percent [of employees in terms of performance] are managed differently. This group of people is enormously valuable to any company; you simply cannot function without their skills, energy, and commitment. After all, they are the majority of your employees. But everyone in the middle 70 needs to be motivated, and made to feel as if they truly belong. You do not want to lose the vast majority of your middle 70—you want to improve them."

—Jack Welch, *Winning*[7]

Social architecture doesn't require a public figure like Welch to be enormously effective. In fact, GE's talent management methods continue to evolve and set industry standards more than 10 years after Welch's retirement.

Some of the most successful companies in the world have had a succession of "quiet" CEOs. Johnson & Johnson, for example, expresses its values in "Our Credo," a statement that describes its responsibilities to doctors, nurses, patients, families, employees, communities, and, finally, shareholders. Outlined are specific behavioral guidelines ("Compensation must be fair and adequate, and working conditions clean, orderly, and safe") that are flexible enough to apply across countries, businesses, and cultures. The details in Our Credo are numerous, but the key concept is responsibility to others, a sense that each person's work has an impact on many others, and that individuals within Johnson & Johnson are accountable for that impact. The Credo has been promoted by every CEO at Johnson & Johnson (and none has encouraged a heroic public persona).

Johnson & Johnson's success illustrates one advantage of scale: the global reinforcement of core values endows them with great power. When a large environment is aligned along just a few values, there is little ambiguity. A hundred signals a day promote their adoption. (Any decent manager or line worker can determine whether a workplace is "clean, orderly, and safe.") Scale adds power, however, only if a large majority of employees express the organization's values in their behavior and are encouraged to notice and appreciate it in their colleagues as well.

At the other end of the size spectrum, the start-up organization also benefits from a deliberate social architecture. Start-ups classically begin with a few people, a vision, and an obsessive focus on just one or two central ideas. That focus is critical when a company is small and the CEO can promote an idea face-to-face with 10 or 50 or 100 employees. But daily interaction with employees for a start-up executive becomes impossible as the company grows. It's just a fact of life. There will be people the CEO won't see on a daily basis, so the cult of personality wanes as the company grows to 50 employees or more.

Zappos.com is a great example of successfully translating the values of a hero CEO deep within an organization as it experiences explosive growth. A key value for Zappos is its nonnegotiable, obsessive, 24/7 devotion to customer service. The company's CEO, Tony Hsieh, built the company around it. (Motto: "At Zappos.com, Customer Service Is Everything. In Fact, It's the Entire Company.") Early on, Tony and his executive team promoted these values by power of example, by asking at every opportunity, "How will this affect the customer?", and by rewarding and recognizing workers who shared the company's obsession with customer satisfaction. As the company grew, Tony and his team hired like-minded managers who demonstrated their passion for customer satisfaction in their actions.[9] Today, the company has sales of more than $1 billion, and each new employee is hired on the basis of its values—putting the customer first—and publicly or privately honored for any demonstration of that value. When Jeff Bezos, Amazon.com's CEO, announced the purchase of Zappos in July 2009, he credited the company's obsession with customer service for his decision. Bezos said that such a company made him "weak in the knees"—to the tune of around $900 million—and added that he wasn't going to change a thing. (Incidentally, Bezos is known to place an empty chair at the table during executive meetings—a chair that stands for the customer.)

Executive Insight

"What he [Hsieh] really cares about is making Zappos.com's employees and customers feel really, really good because he has decided that his entire business revolves around one thing: happiness. Everything at Zappos.com serves that end.

"Zappos.com's 1,300 employees talk about the place with a religious fervor. The phrase core values can prompt emotional soliloquies, and the CEO is held with a regard typically afforded rock stars and cult leaders."[10]

—Max Chafkin, Inc. Magazine

Three components of social architecture deserve special mention here: shared values, employee engagement, and united execution create a high-performance culture. Social recognition is the link connecting all three.

Shared Values

Management teams spend countless hours concisely defining their company's values into a cultural vision that inspires employees to achieve strategic goals. Ideally, values should also differentiate a company from its competitors. In reality, it is difficult to move these values beyond the engraved plaque hanging on the wall, as we've seen, and even more difficult to sustain a shared appreciation of the values day in, day out.

Unity matters. For a company's values to have an impact on employee behavior and performance, they must be understood in the same way by all employees regardless of position, division, geographic location, or tenure with the company.

The company's unique value set needs to be promoted, rewarded, and propagated.

Shared values are taught, retaught, and honored when recognition draws attention to specific behaviors tied to a company value. The individual being recognized is reminded of the value's importance. If the recognition is public within the company, the importance of behaviors and values is magnified for everyone to see. If all recognition within a set time is shared in a team meeting, then entire teams will be reminded of the company's values. (In large, globally distributed companies this is the only efficient way to make the company values come alive for every employee.)

To achieve this level of common understanding, managers must communicate the organization's values with a unified understanding of what each value means and its importance. However, this task can be diluted not only by a company's scale but also by a varied and diverse workforce (especially in global companies). Furthermore, the task of communicating is complicated by variability in communication skills among managers and by individual managers' perceptions of the relative worth of certain values. To manage is to choose among multiple options, and business situations inevitably cause a manager to choose in the moment between, for example, customer satisfaction and greater efficiency. Deeply ingrained values point the way to resolve these conflicting options.

Organizations that value their culture should recruit people who are likely to behave in the way that expresses that culture. In an article in the *New York Times*, reporter Claire Cain Miller described the hiring system at Zappos:

"Employees go through two sets of interviews, one about qualifications and one to see if they fit the culture. All employees work in the call center for a month. After a week, they can take the pay they have earned plus $2,000 and leave."[11]

Zappos wants committed people so much that it will pay those who don't feel like they fit to leave! And that makes great business sense when you consider the low productivity (and drag on morale) of a non-engaged employee.

Hiring to Fit the Company Culture

Deliberate management decisions, not happenstance, create a high-performance culture. For employees, this begins with the hiring process.

Fairmont Hotels & Resorts, another splendid example of effective hiring, spends a lot of time and money during its hiring process to identify and confirm a candidate's dedication to outstanding service. Fairmont looks for employees who want to delight hotel guests. This requires hard-to-measure qualities like empathy, creativity, and spontaneity. Matt Smith, Fairmont's Vice President of Talent and Learning, gives this example of a successful hire:

"We had guests staying with us in one of our resorts in the Rocky Mountains in a room that had a big stone fireplace. As they left the room to go swimming, one of their children said, 'Mom, I can't believe there's a fireplace. Do you think they'll know how much I love marshmallows? Could we roast marshmallows?' Well, a room attendant—the person cleaning the room—happened to overhear that conversation. When the family returned, they found a basket of marshmallows, graham crackers, and chocolates, all to make s'mores, around the fire. On the basket was a little handwritten note from the employee saying, 'Because we know how much you like marshmallows.'

"You can't engineer that kind of creativity," adds Matt. "You can't write a manual that says, 'If you ever have a kid and a fireplace, send marshmallows.' What you *can* do is recognize the magic that spontaneous, creative service creates, and keep hiring people who want to make that magic. And you can manage a continuous process of turning those unpredictable moments into organizational culture, through appreciation, communication, and celebration of those acts."

Engagement and Social Architecture

We've discussed the business reasons to cultivate engaged employees. There is a cultural reason as well: an engaged employee is a cornerstone of social architecture.

If a spirit of innovation is a core cultural value, for example, then any time an employee suggests a new way of doing things, or a creative idea for a product or service, he or she is demonstrating that value. That's engagement—going beyond the letter of the job and promoting one value that makes up company culture. When others recognize, celebrate, and appreciate individual acts of innovation, that value is reinforced socially.

To dramatize how engagement creates and reinforces healthy social architecture, imagine the opposite: In a workplace where people are just doing their jobs, not really interested in giving more, neither energized nor attached nor promoting values, social architecture is brittle scaffolding. Who cares about a spirit of innovation if nobody notices?

Robert Levering, founder of the Great Place to Work Institute®, says that trust has three components. "Let's say you're the manager and I'm the employee. The first component is, what do I think about you? Do I think you have integrity, and that you are reliable? The second component of trust is fairness. . . . It's important that the basic deal we've got is fair; it's not just important what I think about you, it's what *I think you think about me.*

"The third component of trust is respect, and the most important aspect of respect is whether or not you show appreciation for what I do. . . . In the workplace, that's *the* central element of showing respect."[12]

Integrity, fairness, respect: If you want to promote trust in the workplace (and you should), these three components have to be part of your social architecture. Otherwise you will have disengaged employees and your social architecture will be a house of cards.

Culture Drift

We often observe *culture drift* in customers' workplaces. Although a company's values are appropriate to the business, they aren't reinforced or adapted to meet changing business conditions. The bright-eyed, curious, and energetic qualities of engagement have become bogged down in habit.

Company goals, objectives, and even strategies can (and should) change over time. But the underlying company culture and supporting values likely will not. The culture and values are all about *how* the work gets done—how employees behave with each other, the customers, and others to accomplish the mission.

The Globoforce 2012 Fall Workforce Mood Tracker (a semi-annual survey of key workforce topics) found that 95 percent of employees who receive recognition based on company values say they feel enabled to achieve the company's objectives. Reminding employees every day, in every position, of these values through positive, purposeful recognition keeps your culture from drifting into dangerous waters.

A strong social architecture supports all forms of engagement because the community rewards valuable behaviors day by day. Little improvements are called out for praise. Big initiatives are greeted with excitement. Goodwill expands, trust and appreciation grow, and the power of thanks becomes an emotional benefit among employees at all levels. In this way, over time, the social architecture of a company helps make engagement self-sustaining. Instead of a heroic CEO continuously admonishing people to "get in the game," the community of employees is itself powering the culture.

Writing on the Globoforce blog, Susan Piver (author of the bestselling *Hard Questions* book series) described the behaviors that characterize an atmosphere of engagement in a corporate culture:

"People feel engaged not when they are agreed with, but when they are listened to. People feel engaged when they are acknowledged. Acknowledgement doesn't mean praising or agreeing. It simply means taking an interest in the other person's point of view and offering a clear response. If you find it praiseworthy, an interesting conversation can arise. If you find it off-target, a different interesting conversation can happen. If it makes you angry, upset, delighted, or confused—these too can be interesting. Nothing is off limits and people feel trusted and appreciated.

"Openness and trust . . . come from connecting, person to person, over and over, and sustaining that connection when there is agreement and when there is confusion."[13]

Living Culture: JetBlue

Anne Rhoades, the creator of JetBlue's People Team, recalls how the airline's interest in safety caused her to hire a mechanic no other company would touch:

"I asked one of the first technicians we hired, 'Give me an example of a time when safety was an issue but it was a very difficult thing to own up to because you knew that your superior did not agree.' He said, 'I graduated at the top of my class and went to work for a New York airline, a job I had wanted all my life. About sixty days into the job, we had a plane going overseas I did not feel was perfectly safe. There were two or three items I thought we should fix before I signed off. I went to my supervisor, and he said that I needed to sign off without the fixes.' "

Anne continues: "He didn't sign off and got fired. No other airline would touch him. We hired him because he put his career on the line for a safety issue. That shows incredible integrity. He's now a supervisor at JetBlue."

United Execution

Ultimately, social architecture's value is to drive behaviors that support the company's mission and business goals. This requires united execution, which means that individuals function as a team, supporting each other's individual activities and goals as well as performing their own. Even if individuals share most company values and cultural beliefs, without united execution they risk error, mistrust, and miscommunication. Friendly rivalries and competition for rewards and distinctions (as in sales contests) depend on united execution, too. If someone cheats or undermines his or her colleagues, people quickly adapt with all the dysfunctional behaviors one sees in an unhealthy culture (backstabbing, unspoken rivalries, withholding support).

With united execution, competition for rewards remains rule-bound and fair. People support and encourage each other because they understand that the larger goals they share benefit everyone.

As individuals and teams unite in execution of projects large and small, they earn the power to assume self-management. They brainstorm, critique, solve problems, and create solutions without constant prodding from a manager. The social architecture is built strong with every positive interaction and is built right when all work is directed ultimately at a shared strategic goal.

At the extreme end of the need for teamwork (in the military, professional sports teams, or intense turnaround situations, for example) united execution is vital, and everyone knows it. At that extreme you will invariably hear people say, "I'm doing it for the team" or "We're all in this together," and they'll mean it. Some of the best moments of our professional lives take place at the times when circumstances compel all to unite in execution. Imagine if that happened all the time.

Shared values, engaged employees, and united execution can be a daily reality with a strong, supportive, and inclusive social architecture. Strong social architecture, like the architecture of houses or cathedrals, is born of long thought and careful planning and deliberate work. And it requires specialized tools to come into being.

The tools that work best for building social architecture are the different forms of recognition. That set of tools is the subject of Chapter 5.

5 | The Evolution and Reinvention of Recognition

Symantec is a Fortune 500 company providing data security, storage, and systems management solutions. In 2008, the company faced a problem all too common in successful tech firms: A major acquisition doubled the workforce overnight, from 6,500 to 14,000 employees, and that scale of change created uncertainty. Employees joining the company were anxious to understand their new role in the larger organization, and long-term employees wondered if expansion would change Symantec's culture.

HR and top leadership discovered that Symantec was becoming a "culture of cultures"—a potential muddle of values and habits that could threaten its effectiveness in a business demanding united execution and shared priorities. The situation posed a threat of great talent going unrecognized, becoming disaffected, and potentially leaving the company. As with most mergers, communication issues and cultural conflict had the potential to derail the value of a unified business.

Company leadership needed a program to unify the company behind its core values of trust, action, and innovation and get everyone aligned behind a shared vision. A recognition practice could potentially bring people together, but at the time, different business units ran a variety of old-fashioned recognition programs. Ironically, the world-class data protection company did not have the data needed to measure the impact of recognition dollars spent.

Needing to unify its vastly expanded workforce with one culture and one employee brand, Symantec implemented a social recognition practice aligned with its own sophisticated use of data. HR requirements included delivering data-driven workforce insight to senior leadership.

Defining a long-term social recognition strategy and journey (versus an uncoordinated array of tactical recognition tools) resulted in a measurable behavior and cultural change at Symantec.

Senior executives threw their support fully behind the program, called Applause—and they required measurable results. Nine months after launching Applause, Symantec's employee satisfaction scores were up 14 percent. That's the kind of number any company could appreciate, even in a time of rocketing growth.

The Social Recognition Journey

In the days of lifelong employment and strict hierarchies, HR professionals trained managers to expect performance and provide encouragement. Managers balanced carrots (rewards) and sticks (consequences, which typically meant withholding rewards). That seemed sufficient when employers believed peak performance required only training, command, and compensation.

Those days are gone. Today's employees seek self-determination. Lifelong employment is a thing of the past, and, in response, the best talents in your company think of themselves as "temporary workers"— engaged not out of loyalty to the company but because their needs for both tangible and psychic income are satisfied. They want their work to have meaning, not just monetary reward. Effective managers know this and use tactical recognition to teach and bond with the employees they must guide day-to-day.

The practice of recognition evolved over recent decades as the relationship between managers and staff came under closer scrutiny. Recognition and appreciation began to be directly connected to company values and goals. Practiced across entire companies, recognition flattened the emotional hierarchy of the corporation just as other social habits, like addressing a company officer by his first name, became more flexible and less formal. At the same time, recognition grew in sophistication.

Today, recognition is a full-featured management practice. Like employer branding and financial management, it is a set of actions, rules, and processes working together to achieve strategic goals. And like other management practices, recognition ranges from simple, tactical steps through enterprise-wide initiatives to long-term strategic practices. The progress of an organization from simple to sophisticated practice is the *recognition journey* we mentioned in the Introduction. A compelling quality of recognition is that it works even at a small scale, and its benefits magnify as the recognition journey progresses.

> *Today, recognition is a full-featured management practice.*

Figure 5.1 shows the progress through different levels of recognition. Each column describes a more sophisticated and powerful program because it incorporates increasingly sophisticated practices. Most of our customers come to us with *tactical recognition*—spot recognition programs handled by supervisors on an ad hoc basis. *Enterprise recognition* reaches every part of a company around the globe with a consistent program. *Strategic recognition* adds a greater emphasis on culture management, connecting recognition with company values and long-term strategic goals as positivity begins to flow with the work across the organization. *Social recognition* takes advantage of the behavioral habits and the new social technologies to involve everyone in the process

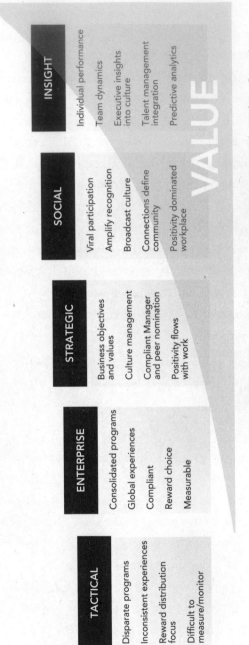

TACTICAL

Disparate programs

Inconsistent experiences

Reward distribution focus

Difficult to measure/monitor

ENTERPRISE

Consolidated programs

Global experiences

Compliant

Reward choice

Measurable

STRATEGIC

Business objectives and values

Culture management

Compliant Manager and peer nomination

Positivity flows with work

SOCIAL

Viral participation

Amplify recognition

Broadcast culture

Connections define community

Positivity dominated workplace

INSIGHT

Individual performance

Team dynamics

Executive insights into culture

Talent management integration

Predictive analytics

VALUE

BIG DATA | TECHNOLOGIES: Analytics, Mobile, Web, Video, Security

Figure 5.1 Social recognition journey

of recognition. Connections made in social recognition help define and even create community among employees, becoming truly Positivity Dominated Workplaces. The ultimate step on the journey is to use the ever more sophisticated analysis of recognition data to gain detailed *insight* into the workforce's performance, combining behavior data with financial and other management data to show how certain behaviors drive results.

Underlying the journey is an evolving foundation of ever-greater technological power. *Mobile recognition* makes recognition available any-time, anywhere, through a secure interface into the social recognition platform via any smartphone device. Video components put a more inti-mate and familiar face onto recognition moments, just as video calling and messaging have done with mobile communications. Advances in security protect the information of a company and its employees. "Big Data" analytics project the power of recognition into new areas of talent management (see Chapter 8).

Traditional, tactical recognition programs—the ones we often see when new customers tell us their recognition is producing mediocre results—fall short of their worthy goals because they have not adapted to the changes in business culture, structure, and management practices. The recognition program that places plastic "awards" on cubicle walls should have gone the way of the typewriter by now.

To understand the recognition journey, let's first see how and why recognition works.

Motivation, Incentives, and Recognition

The foundational idea behind all recognition is that employees pro-duce the best results when they are motivated to engage fully with their work, and the operating principle of motivation is incentive. In purely psychological terms, motivation is an emotional state, and incentive is the stimulus that gives rise to that state.

When we speak of a motivated employee, we imagine someone ener-gized and engaged in his or her job. Break down the idea of motivation, and you'll realize that it comes in two forms: *extrinsic motivation*, in which someone works to gain an external reward like cash or a promotion, and *intrinsic motivation*, in which someone works to gain a personal sense of achievement or control over his or her choices and environment, a positive state psychologists call *agency*.

Extrinsic motivation requires continuous refreshment of tangible external rewards—last year's bonus won't motivate this year's behavior; only the prospect of another bonus will do that. Intrinsic motivation requires less immediate prompting but flourishes in an environment that enables achievement and agency on an ongoing basis.

When we speak of incentives in a business setting, we generally mean those that encourage extrinsic motivation—pay, bonuses, benefits, cool technology, a pleasant working environment, or prestige in the form of an impressive job title. These are forms of recognition, but recognition as a practice also includes intrinsically oriented rewards, as shown in Figure 5.2.

The important distinction between recognition and incentives is the focus or intent of the program. Recognition focuses on the *how*—the behaviors demonstrated to accomplish desired results. Incentives focus more purely on rewarding the *what*—the results achieved. Daniel Pink, author of *Drive: The Surprising Truth About What Motivates Us* and *To Sell Is Human*, further explains the difference in terms of the surprise

RECOGNITION focuses on the HOW	INCENTIVES focus on the WHAT
Subjective behavior	Quantifiable business goals
Unknown reward (surprises)	Programmatic rewards
Spontaneous: Unexpected	Programmed: known time intervals
Emotional value first	Extrinsic value: known reward
Monetary value secondary	Intrinsic value: ranking among peers
Values-based	Metrics-based
Focused on many winners	Reward the top, move the middle

Figure 5.2 Recognition and incentives

and expectation factor of rewards. Incentives are given in the spirit of "If/Then"—"If you do X, then you'll receive Y." The target result is fully prescribed (often encouraging people to achieve precisely that result and no more), and the reward is expected and known beforehand. Recognition, on the other hand, is more focused on "Now/That" rewards—"Now that you've demonstrated or achieved X, here is a surprise reward Y." There is no preestablished expectation of reward, encouraging employees to continuously pursue goals beyond expectations.

Expert Insight

"Recognition matters. A lot. Because recognition acknowledges the progress people need, frequently catch people in the act of making progress, call it out so people notice it, share it more widely and formally, and celebrate it. This is so powerful because Mastery depends on feedback. This kind of Now/That recognition is a powerful form of feedback. If it's non-contingent (not held out as a carrot), it's very motivating to Mastery . . ."[1]

—Dan Pink, author of *Drive: The Surprising Truth About What Motivates Us*

The broadest, most adaptable set of rewards for business creates a balance of extrinsic and intrinsic motivation. This means combining incentives and recognition. An employer doesn't have to choose between extrinsic or intrinsic motivations, or between incentives and recognition. Choosing both, implementing both, and treating both as vital practices yields the best program. A broad program of culture management contains known rewards (year-end bonuses) with unknown rewards (spontaneous recognition). An enterprise compensation plan can include a customized reward program for an elite few (e.g., stock ownership) and recognition programs for all.

Total Rewards

The HR concept of total rewards understands that cash is a necessary but incomplete component of compensation. The baseline relationship of employer and employee is a contract: cash in the form of salary, benefits, and bonuses in return for performing the tasks in a job description. On both sides of that contract there is a lot of variability in performance. Some employees regularly go beyond their job descriptions; some workplaces are rich with intangible rewards. Every employer wants a workforce made up of such employees, and employees (especially the best ones) respond to employers who go beyond the minimum compensations.

The goal of total rewards is to achieve the highest return on investment with the optimal mix of rewards. In practice, managers calibrate and apply this menu of rewards to attract, motivate, engage, and retain employees individually. That leads directly to improved performance and business results. High-performing companies have figured this out. They also know what studies have shown for decades: noncash factors like work-life balance, a sense of mission, and manager appreciation are more flexible and adaptable methods of motivating employees than simply increasing salaries.

Recognition has an additional advantage over cash in a total rewards strategy. To state the obvious: there is a limit to the cash compensation that sound financial management will allow. While a recognition practice has a cost, its appeal to intrinsic motivation magnifies its impact in a qualitatively different manner than cash. As part of an optimal mix of rewards, recognition is a highly efficient motivator. And it's much cheaper than spiraling salaries.

Roger Martin, former dean of the Rotman School of Management at the University of Toronto and coauthor of *Playing to Win: How Strategy Really Works*, recently shared these thoughts about the relationship between compensation and recognition with Globoforce:

"Organizations spend far too much time and energy on compensation and not nearly enough on recognition. People long to be a valued member of their organization and want to feel that it is a meritorious place—the latter because it helps them feel that it is worth being a valuable member of it. Both require recognition. Workers need to know that they are valued and they will feel better if they are working for a company that values its employees in a thorough and intelligent fashion.

"The dominant tool organizations use for this purpose is monetary compensation. It is an expensive, blunt-edged, and frankly pretty crummy tool. It is smarter to have a variety of ways of recognizing employees. There is a reason why school kids love gold stars even though they cost almost nothing. They make them feel like valuable members of their class community. That is the goal of intelligent recognition."[2]

> "Monetary compensation is an expensive, blunt-edged, and frankly pretty crummy tool [for recognition]."

Cash Versus Noncash Rewards

As a tool for recognition, cash has drawbacks. Place an extra $100 in a biweekly paycheck, and an employee might not even notice. And even those who do notice will connect that award with the paycheck—what's expected and what's exceptional get bundled together.

Make that same $100 award in the form of a choice of gift cards, given on the spot with public recognition for going beyond the job description, and the whole nature of the award changes. It's unexpected and spontaneous. It's a delightful surprise. The employee might use it for an impulse purchase, a treat, a gift for a loved one, even a contribution to a local charity like a holiday clothing drive.

MYTHBUSTER
"If it's free, it's forgotten."

Making recognition "free" in the sense that it carries no tangible reward is a tempting concept. Why not just give someone a "thumbs-up" in an e-mail? It sounds good in theory, because the act does imply genuine goodwill, but in our experience there are two fatal problems with this approach.

Serious organizational programs always involve investments of time, effort, and money. Programs a company does not back with investment are de facto second- or third-class programs, and every employee knows it. Our shorthand for this problem is, "If it's free, it's forgotten."

While managers might initially like the idea that recognition costs nothing, they subtly assign it little value. Once managers leave the recognition seminar and go back to their desks, they look at the folders and e-mails and schedules piled up and start prioritizing their tasks, and recognition falls to the bottom of the to-do list once again.

Employees have the last word on "free" recognition: in a 2014 Globoforce Workforce Mood Tracker survey, only 4 percent of employees stated "eThanks" with no lasting economic value in the form of a noncash reward were memorable.[3]

A gift associated with your "thanks" is much more engaging, personal, and meaningful—and it is directly associated with engagement. Done right, the award has been publicly connected with a behavior specifically connected with a company value like cost containment or customer service. Done *expertly*, the award is at the center of a narrative story told by an employee's manager as an example of the kind of behavior that management appreciates. An award with just $100 in gift value thus produces many other forms of value and appeals to the intrinsic motivators of pride and gratification at the manager's genuine expression of gratitude.

As an additional benefit, the noncash tangible award can be more memorable than cash. If I use a gift card to purchase a sweater, every time I wear that sweater I'm reminded of the award and its surrounding narrative of engagement in my work, positive relations with my boss, pride, and sense of accomplishment. If I use it for an experience like dinner with my significant other, the memory of that dinner is more "sticky" than the memory of an extra $100 in my paycheck. It extends the recognition moment.

From a budgeting point of view as well, noncash awards are efficient uses of a budget. The same $5,000 can appear as one person's annual bonus, or it can pay for 50 on-the-spot awards with an economic value of $100 to 10 employees over the course of a year. For the same investment, you get much more strategic, lasting impact.

Cash has its place, but it's only at high enough award levels that the award doesn't get lost in a paycheck. As we shall see, there are cases when cash awards are appropriate in a recognition program, but on the whole, noncash awards have significant advantages over cash. First and foremost, noncash awards at multiple differentiated lower levels (ranging in economic value from $25/$50 to $1,000, or their points equivalent) are, as stated above, a better use of recognition budget while also a means to encourage the recipient to select a reward that might be a bit of a splurge. If given as cash through payroll at these lower levels, the award tends to be used as part of the recipient's regular budget for groceries or gas—not the memorable experiential reward. However, cash awards above $2,000 certainly do not get lost in a paycheck, and the necessary fanfare around more rare awards of this size will ensure the long-lasting memory of the cash award.

Measure It!

One more principle applies to recognition at any stage in the journey: the need to measure how many acts of recognition are actually occurring in the organization. Managers should have targets based on the size of their teams and the scope of their challenges. Managers also need a stake in the game; that is, carrying out a recognition program should be part of *their* job descriptions just as much as managing a budget or maintaining quality standards.

Noticing and recognizing extra effort is a habit of some managers but by no means all. For the former, a professional recognition program multiplies their natural strengths. The latter might need convincing and training to see that recognition improves their management effectiveness.

To those who suggest there just isn't enough discretionary effort in their staff to merit a recognition program, there is a simple answer: Why not? It is the manager's job to get the most out of his or her team. In our experience, there are indeed engaged employees in their groups, or at least discretionary effort, but the manager isn't noticing it (or tapping into it fully).

In the case of a low-functioning team, setting a target for recognition moments can help inspire greater engagement and better results. Nobody takes pride in belonging to a losing group or paddling his or her oar in a company backwater. Even little celebrations of small victories—a process improved here, a colleague helped there, a problem solved in a creative or novel manner—can be all it takes for a group to start shaking off the self-fulfilling expectation that nothing will change.

As recognition grows from a few scattered moments to an enterprise-wide and then strategic practice, goodwill grows. People expect more than a reward for a job well done; they create the expectation among themselves of jobs done exceptionally well.

Let's take a deeper look at the recognition journey. It begins with the simplest form of the practice, tactical recognition.

Tactical Recognition

Tactical recognition focuses on the connection between a manager and an individual employee. The manager notices extra effort or good performance and recognizes it with an award and a personal message. If the manager is good at this, she'll also point out why that employee's effort supports company values. (Incidentally, when we say "manager and employee" we mean everyone from line managers to top executives. Recognition works at all levels.)

"Catch them doing something good" is the slogan for this kind of recognition. Proponents focus on the *recognition moment*—the positive interaction between manager and employee. They encourage managers to find many little ways to celebrate employee performance so that positive reinforcement becomes a habit.

The elements of this program are familiar—it is fulfillment-driven, meaning the tangible reward for extra effort is based on a predetermined amount of cash or an item from a catalog (managed by a recognition vendor). There is a budget for awards but little reporting, and often little consistency among an organization's departments and divisions. In a global organization, we have sometimes seen a dozen different recognition programs operating simultaneously. This can result from mergers and acquisitions and might reflect global cultural differences. Reporting and analysis, which could evaluate the value and effectiveness of the program, are all but impossible.

This one-to-one connection has benefits, especially in the hands of emotionally intelligent managers. Most of us have seen managers who just had a knack for recognizing and applauding their people. It's positive effort, and it motivates employees to become more enthusiastic about their jobs. At a company level, the chief appeal of tactical recognition is that it's easy and fun. People like to give and receive a pat on the back. (In fact, it's a sad comment on most corporate cultures that this basic tactical recognition is an improvement on the appreciation employees typically receive, which is very little.)

A tactical recognition program often works best in a small business, which is typically driven by the personality and leadership of the owner. Mallory's Auto Repair, with 10 employees, is a small society in which Mallory can celebrate and recognize good work frequently. GE, with more than 300,000 employees, is a different story. Most employees are part of many layers of management or are thousands of miles removed from executives. Managers with diverse personalities, cultural expectations, and leadership abilities cannot be expected to behave in the same way or convey the same critical messages. An individual recognition program that relies on creative and spontaneous impulse is out of place in the complex, data-dependent multinational corporation. You simply can't deliver this spontaneous behavior across thousands of individuals through hope, encouragement, or cajoling alone.

Effective managers in a global company need to approach recognition the way they approach all practices: with an eye on provable results. In such a workplace, systems need to be in place to encourage the right behavior in the appropriate scale.

A large organization can't depend on the enlightenment of every manager and his or her ability (or willingness) to find 1,000 ways to give trinkets to employees. Furthermore, a large organization risks complete chaos in its recognition efforts if it can't provide a scalable way for all managers to recognize their people. It needs a recognition solution that can scale across the enterprise and also provide a level of corporate governance so the CFO can sleep well at night

Enterprise Recognition

The second stage of the recognition journey is enterprise recognition, which means spreading the practice of tactical recognition across a company's different divisions and functions. Enterprise recognition, like enterprise financial management or procurement practices, establishes standard objectives, practices, ways, and means to accomplish recognition's goals.

In the last few decades, an entire industry grew up to create more formal recognition programs for organizations larger than 100 employees. Recognition companies provided simple guidelines and basic training for managers who might not otherwise know the most effective ways to recognize their people. They offered large catalogs of awards and prizes that managers could give to employees.

This enterprise recognition is the next step in the evolution of a recognition practice. It encourages managers to participate in recognition. It gives some amount of quality control to the people in charge of recognition, typically someone in the human resources department. It makes recognition standard and scalable across big organizations, just as a purchasing department can standardize and scale the buying of office supplies.

What happens when you take a good idea like tactical recognition and try to scale it across the enterprise? Typically, you invest in the supporting structures of a recognition program. You create or buy different tools to scale training, communication, and the physical delivery of awards. You make the program global. You make it sustainable in terms of making sure that everybody has access to the right budgets and it's happening all over the enterprise, in different divisions and in different languages. In short, you add another layer of value to the delivery of tactical recognition to ensure it's delivered company-wide.

However, delivering a company-wide, universally adopted recognition program requires a break from the past in terms of typical program design. Old-fashioned recognition programs are notoriously hard to scale:

- Old-fashioned recognition programs demand creativity from some managers who just don't have it. (Its acolytes try to overcome this problem by promoting lists with names like "365 ways to reward employees.")
- Old-fashioned recognition programs, as typically practiced, focus awards around previously chosen objects, such as a lapel pin, a USB flash drive, a cupcake, a desk set, a Lucite paperweight with the company logo. The value of the gift is subjective and variable according to the recipient's taste and the giver's choice.
- Old-fashioned recognition programs' focus on these objects complicates implementation across cultures in large global companies. The programs tend to be focused on the employees in the country where company headquarters is located and thus fail to account for cultural differences that would demonstrate respect and understanding of employees' local cultures in geographically distributed offices.
- Old-fashioned recognition programs are difficult to manage in terms of directing costs to best use, tracking the business benefits of the practice, and following up. Focused on the individual manager

and the recognition moment, these programs generally rely on ad hoc reporting and subjective impressions.

- Old-fashioned recognition programs, because they require such creativity and depend on manager buy-in, are hard to enforce and typically have low penetration rates.

Enterprise recognition is a more sophisticated approach. However, it is not effortless to launch or to sustain. If you design the program incorrectly at the start, you'll have great difficulty in scaling it up so that it reaches 80 to 90 percent of the workforce. Standardized solutions create friction in a large, complex department. There are logistical issues around ordering and shipping merchandise. People often don't participate because they have never heard of the program or they don't like the awards. In a global organization, there are language, currency, equity, and tax complications.

Enterprise recognition falls short of recognition's true potential because it is layered onto a culture in the same manner as a benefit program. It stays in the human resources silo—a positive step forward, to be sure, but not answerable like other disciplines to management practices of measurement against goals. That represents a huge missed opportunity. There is a much greater potential implementation of recognition that brings all the acts of appreciation and motivation into the most rigorous practices of management, on a par with financial, legal, and operations management. That is the next step on the recognition journey, strategic recognition.

Bring Back the Years-of-Service Award!

A hallmark of old-fashioned recognition programs was the years-of-service award, commemorating 5, 10, 15, 20, and 25 years at a company. They fell out of favor as job tenure shortened, layoffs grew, and longevity lost the respect it once commanded. And the "gold watch" association seemed just too old-style.

It's time to restore and renew the years-of-service award. The key to making it relevant is "crowdsourcing" the recognition narrative by inviting everyone to contribute. When a program allows any employee to recall moments in the career of someone who has been at the company for years, the tremendous impact one person can have becomes brilliantly clear.

Imagine if 25 or 50 people recalled accomplishments by a peer who has been at the company for 20 years; what emerges is a summary history of the company's evolution over those years—changes in products, people who came and went, values that grew more important over time, and positive interactions. As others hear the story of a longtime employee's career, they learn that their relationship to the company can be more than transactional and that their impact can be far greater than the quarterly numbers.

Now imagine the benefit of collecting statements of appreciation from peers over the long term. For an individual, a years-of-service award would include recognition from colleagues old and new from years past and from last week. A timeline narrative of the individual's entire career at the company is at hand, created socially by many people, some of whom might not even be at the company any longer. This collection of heartfelt testimonials confers incredibly powerful meaning to the award. A recognition program, over time, gives the company a large database of such moments, ready to make the milestone award that much more meaningful.

In this way, the community comes together to celebrate its shared work; what was a single award becomes a social experience

As a side benefit, crowdsourced years-of-service awards contribute to institutional memory, reminding current (and even future) employees of the culture and values that carry on through decades of change. That message of continuity transcends short-term thinking and reemphasizes that even a temporary employee is contributing to a larger mission and long-term value. That message makes much greater impact than just recognizing endurance!

Years-of-service awards should be made in the context of a global recognition program, lest others interpret them as favoring longevity over creativity or other notable behaviors. By encouraging a narrative of longtime accomplishment, managers can showcase the unique contributions of longtime employees.

Strategic Recognition

Strategic recognition is the practice of integrating recognition with other management tools and practices, taking recognition beyond the HR domain and leveraging its power to shape behavior at all levels of the organization. Strategic recognition is the point at which the "soft" behaviors of recognition—which worked well at motivating employees—finally merge with the "hard" management practices of measurement, goal-setting, analysis, and strategic execution. At this level, as with so many practices today, new value is realized by unlocking heretofore hidden data.

When many recognition moments across the enterprise are recorded in a database, analyzed, and understood, remarkable patterns appear. Recognition becomes as potent a management tool as financial tracking or supply chain management.

The data of strategic recognition—what awards are being given, to whom, and why—show the degree to which company values are being lived out day to day. Using data visualization tools, HR learns which values are emphasized, by which departments and managers, in which locations, and how often, all in a visual dashboard based on real-time data. These data are interpreted against strategic goals such as engagement, employee satisfaction, or cultural change.

In large organizations, this might mean hundreds of rich new data sets every day. This is a paradigm shift in culture management: actually monitoring values-based performance in detail with data, not just anecdotes.

The data raise the bar on performance when it comes to cultural initiatives. More than once, we've had the conversation with potential customers in which we mention a new cultural idea or slogan promulgated by the C-suite and the branch managers say, "What's that? We've never heard of that." Or even worse, they say, "Yeah, that's the latest slogan from headquarters, but nobody follows up." That kind of disconnect might be inexcusable, but it's all too common in the soft-skills world of culture management. Imagine if those managers were discussing a technology initiative or a new product line!

Technology initiatives and new product lines are supported with a sophisticated reporting protocol and tracking technology because they make a difference to the bottom line. Strategic recognition treats cultural performance with the same level of seriousness and support because it too makes a difference to the bottom line. (Like the best initiatives, strategic recognition also is self-improving: The data it supplies support the implementation of recognition itself, holding leaders accountable for their use of recognition as a management technique.)

Because tracking and monitoring tools are in place, practitioners use strategic recognition to manage the culture in detail. For example, HR can alert managers to put more emphasis on a particular value, such as innovation, that the company needs to meet its objectives. If an economic downturn forces a midyear shift to containing costs and hanging onto customers, managers can instantly and continuously call out moments when employees do just that, educating and encouraging everyone to shift their emphasis from the previous priorities (energetic growth) to the current situation (surviving the storm). In this situation, recognition supports a strategic change instantly, continuously, and for as long as it takes to succeed.

Research Insight

"For most companies, recognition is an underutilized asset,
one that you can—and should—set on the right track. Your
recognition programs telegraph what you value and what you
want to happen; recognition is how your employees perceive
what they are supposed to do. So if you're unsure of whether
your message—or strategic plan, or shift in culture—is getting
through, a well-run recognition program can tell you."

—Carol Pletcher, "Beyond the
Handshake," *The Conference Board
Review*, Fall 2009

The promise of strategic recognition is thus multilayered and multidimensional.

- For the employee, it teaches the connection between behavior and values; it increases morale and encourages engagement, loyalty, and attachment.
- For the manager, it compels thinking about which behaviors actually embody company values. This is new, for while it's easy to like certain behaviors, the manager must actually choose which employee actions deserve recognition. To manage is to get work done through others and to choose which behaviors to reinforce. It makes the manager more effective, more accountable, and more directed.
- For the executive, strategic recognition finally—finally!—makes a direct connection between encouraging certain values and knowing if and where those values are being lived by employees and managers. It brings the long-mysterious gifts of "people skills" and the proven need for "hard data" together, ending the unnecessary but persistent conflict between the "humanist" and "realist" schools of management.

Strategic recognition promises to help companies gain competitive advantage, foster employee engagement, improve performance, and increase profits. In a business world growing increasingly interdependent, with organizations growing less command-driven all the time, it is the supple and powerful new way to enrich and manage culture. Strategic recognition is more than a technique; it is a mission.

Expert Insight

"The powerful thing about recognition is that it reminds people of what matters most. This is a key part of engagement—to redirect employee effort and attention to the top priorities of the organization. Regular recognition throughout the year is a reminder of what you need employees to keep doing."

> —Mary Ann Masarech, Employee
> Engagement Practice Manager,
> BlessingWhite[4]

The Final Steps in the Journey

Achieving strategic recognition is a tremendous step, and a company can reap the benefits of that level for a long time, creating new value from every aspect of the program, whether it's single recognition moments or data visualization of a 50,000-member workforce. There are two more steps, or stages of value, in the recognition journey.

Social recognition is a new phenomenon made possible by the rise of Internet social technologies. It's an important development—so great a change that we've devoted the next chapter entirely to social recognition and its implications. It reaches beyond the manager or even the immediate hierarchical team to involve an individual's entire work circle—the people he or she interacts with on a regular basis, past colleagues who have moved to new positions in the organization, and anyone whom the individual wants to keep in touch with through the positive power of thanks. These connections effectively define work communities (and a social recognition system can map these relationships). From a practice standpoint, the community itself is a messenger, broadcasting company culture most fully throughout your organization.

> *Social recognition reaches beyond an employee's manager to give anyone the positive power of thanks.*

Mobile recognition feeds the power of social recognition by ensuring the vast majority of employees, regardless of location or job type, can fully participate in the recognition program through their mobile devices (typically smartphones). The "access anywhere, anytime" availability of mobile today also helps ensure recognition moments are timely and occur very soon after the event deserving of recognition. And since the mobile application is merely another secure interface to the same recognition program, all activity is included in the reporting methodology. Social and mobile technologies together constitute an entire new medium at work, which we explore in Chapter 6.

Insight is our term for the ultimate goal of the recognition journey, in which the practice of social recognition is integrated to all the talent management practices beyond culture management. The key to insight is the capability of today's data analysis technologies to record, interpret, and make connections among the many activities labeled "talent management." A social recognition practice produces analytical tools to give insight to performance assessment, team dynamics, culture management, and other strategic practices such as predictive analytics. Throughout this book you'll see references to social recognition's impact on general management, and its influence on HR topics is a big enough topic that we've devoted Chapter 9 entirely to the implications of insight, the final step in the recognition journey.

Internet technologies have profoundly changed talent management, from job applications to the tools of social media. Just a few years ago, few HR managers had even heard of LinkedIn, Twitter, or Tumblr, and now they are powerful recruiting tools. In Chapter 6, we'll look at how technology and changing habits hold promise and pitfalls for management by recognition.

6 Social, Mobile, and 24/7

The Hershey Company is a growing, global enterprise that connects its approximately 13,000 employees with four core values: *One Hershey, Making a Difference, Growing Together,* and *Open to Possibilities.* Thirteen thousand employees is a large company and Hershey's global reach adds to the complexity. The Hershey Company markets its products in approximately 70 countries worldwide, bridging multiple languages, cultures, and product categories.

Results of the company's global employee survey indicated that workers were looking for a way to recognize their teammates both near and far. So they set out to develop a 24/7, global, social program that would celebrate their values and honor those who go above and beyond in their contributions to the company's success.

The company also needed to identify the program with a symbol meaningful to any employee and connected to its vision. Partnering with Globoforce, the Hershey team created "SMILES."

Traditionally, Human Resources is the only function responsible for recognition. Prior to implementing this new social recognition program, The Hershey Company had dozens of disconnected recognition initiatives varying widely in participation and impact. Hershey rebooted recognition through a partnership between the Total Rewards team in HR and the Quality Through Engagement (QTE) network, which is Hershey's global network focused on driving engagement through appreciating, connecting and empowering all Hershey employees.

The group set out to implement recognition that could reach any employee, anywhere, at any time. They wanted full understanding of the data made possible through social recognition, and they committed to integrating a recognition program into all their engagement methods and technologies. As Kevin Walling, Chief Human Resources Officer, said, "What's great about the SMILES program is that it acknowledges the fact that most of our work now is across the globe and we're working with diverse teams all across Hershey. This is the perfect vehicle to recognize a teammate across the ocean, across the country and even across the office. There's an app on your phone, plus access on your computer. It's now so simple for every employee to recognize great talent and great work across the entire company."

Represented by a smiling HERSHEY'S KISSES silhouette, the Hershey SMILES global recognition program reached employees from the corporate offices in Hershey, Pennsylvania, to sales teams and manufacturing floors around the world. Along with Hershey SMILES posters, badge clips, luggage tags and an online campaign kick-off, the Human Resources Business Partners and QTE network activated ambassadors around the world to host launch day events featuring smiling cupcakes, photo booths, tutorials and more. Eight hundred recognition moments took place in the program's first week, and 14,000 occurred in the first three months, leading to 40 percent of all employees participating in just the first 90 days–halfway toward their goal of 80 percent reach in year one. On mobile devices and at any time, peers can make each other smile with the power of thanks.

Future-Proof Recognition

If you feel buffeted by the pace of change in workforce management, fasten your seat belt. We're at the leading edge of four tectonic trends that are changing employee thinking, behavior, and expectations at an ever-accelerating rate. The workforce is becoming more global, multigenerational, social, and mobile. In a fifth trend, employers are borrowing from consumer technologies to design new systems of employee management.

HR leaders consider these trends when contemplating recognition programs because recognition takes time, investment and training. Protecting those investments means "future-proofing" a recognition program so it will remain relevant to employees five and 10 years from now.

Fortunately, most recognition science is based on permanent human desires and behavior, like craving and expressing appreciation. What *does* change, much faster than human nature, is technology and the business strategies it enables. Any recognition solution worth the name should be flexible enough to change with new and emerging technologies. More specifically, a future-proof recognition solution must be capable of adjusting to new expectations brought on by those technologies or, indeed, anticipate and lead the change itself. To appreciate the power of changing expectations, imagine searching the web today using a browser, computer, and search engine from 1994 or 2004; the wait for a result would seem like an eternity compared to today's technologies, and the quality of that result would elicit a chuckle compared to today's results.

At the same time, the macro-trends in workforce management can't be answered with just an array of new bells and whistles. In a recent report, Gartner analyst Yvette Cameron recommended that HR professionals "look for design flexibility to meet different organizational objectives, including the ability to align all recognition programs— incentive, spot, milestone and others—under a unified program for the greatest impact and budgetary control."[1]

Be mindful of these five trends as you consider a recognition solution, because they will change recognition, and much more of your management tool kit, in the near future.

Business Is Global

Your customers, marketplace, and employees (or potential employees) are paradoxically more widespread in miles yet closer in mindset than they have ever been. Knowledge and information workers are especially conscious that they live in a globalized, 24/7 world of work, information, and entertainment.

Is your organization multinational or global? The difference will predict how complicated a recognition solution will be. A *multinational organization* has locations or facilities in multiple countries, but each location functions in its own way, essentially as its own entity. Multinational recognition might contain a grab bag of solutions managed locally, and while this can be culturally appropriate, it's inefficient and costly.

A *global organization* also has locations in multiple countries, but as far as culture is concerned, its managers have figured out how to create one business culture with one set of processes that facilitate a more efficient and effective single global organization. Global recognition operates on one efficient platform that adjusts for all the different cultural and business factors marking the difference among locations and cultures.

For one example, consider the issue of equity in global companies: Different pay scales, costs of living, and exchange rates mean that an award of moderate monetary value in the United States might be too large in Mexico but too small in Sweden. In addition, tangible awards have broadly different value and meaning in different cultures. More than one U.S. merchandise-based awards program has inadvertently offended non-U.S. recipients of awards. A social recognition practice has to take cultural and economic differences into account to be equitable and effective.

Global organizations have operated on a "think globally, act locally" basis for decades, but with the rise of global social networking on services like Facebook and LinkedIn, and global search engines like Google, that expression has acquired subtle new meaning. Customers (and employees) expect a global service to adapt to local cultures, languages, tastes, and habits. A social recognition practice must reflect how business relationships are conducted locally and still focus on its intended purpose. For example, the Chinese concept of *mianzi* (often translated as "face logic") implies inviting others to share in a positive collective identity and strengthen social relationships. Social recognition is typically understood and adopted quickly in China, where mutual trust, regard, and respect are highly valued, but the right system will deemphasize excess ceremony and emphasize a recipient's connection to the overall goals and values of the team. It will also be designed to make recipients feel not that they must reciprocate recognition in kind (traditional in China), but to "pay it forward" by recognizing others' performance.

In social recognition, thinking globally and acting locally is absolutely necessary, but that doesn't mean it's easy. It takes a comprehensive program including the right technology and the right global knowledge to work.

The breakdown of time barriers is another consequence of our information-saturated world. Thanks to smartphones, tablets, and the global cascade of Internet information, people are habitually plugged into what's going on moment by moment. Even employees who value work-life balance are habituated to answering e-mail and checking Twitter feeds and all the rest at any hour. Work activities and private life seep into each other. Barriers of time and place grow flexible, partly by habit and partly by expectation. A system feature like a secure online recognition news feed is compatible with this trend.

In a 24/7, borderless work world, recognition can potentially happen at any time and any place. In a global organization, recognition of an individual can resonate from Boise to Bangalore, with a consistent message reinforcing engagement, company culture, and shared values. A recognition solution should take advantage of the collapse of time and space and also be compatible with any employee's preferred sense of work-life balance.

Globalizing the Power of Thanks

Globoforce's Content Analyst Darcy Jacobson comments on the subtleties of making recognition work across cultures in a global enterprise:

"It's not the need to be appreciated that changes across borders; it's the way recognition reflects local culture. For example,

a recognition message given to someone in China that emphasizes a specific individual success and personal advancement will
be much less effective than one which instead shows the connection between the employee's work and the overall success of the
team, and emphasizes the achievement within a context of shared
values and goals."

We must have a clear handle on the cultural factors that
affect recognition's language as well. Brandeis professor Andy
Molinsky, in his book *Global Dexterity*, names six variables that
might affect how recognition is expressed. They are directness,
enthusiasm, formality, assertiveness, self-promotion, and personal disclosure.[2] To generalize for the sake of example: In the
United States, recognition might be best expressed directly, with
energy and enthusiasm, whereas in China, the most effective recognition might be styled more indirectly and formally.

Social recognition works best when its reach is global, but its
language is local.

Business Is Multigenerational

The workplace has hosted multiple generations since the days of appren-
ticeships, but today's multigenerational workforce structure is mapped
to a fluid set of criteria based on skills and expertise, not only seniority.
The Great Recession forced many baby boomers (born 1946–1964) to
delay retirement around the time that 40 million members of the millennial generation (born 1980–2000) stepped into the workforce, squeezing
Generation X (born 1965–1980) as that middle cohort advanced to their
prime earning years.[3] (Globally, other demographic and economic forces,
such as China's massive expansion of its middle class, also created multigenerational organizations.) These and changing standards of skills and
experience have brought three generations together as peers, rather than
in the strict hierarchy that once dictated a worker's place.

> *Today, as many as three distinct generations*
> *work side by side as peers.*

Like global organizations, multigenerational workforces succeed when a single set of cultural values unites people in their work while accommodating people's differing needs. For example, an employee in the middle generation, with young children, might value a flexible work schedule more than a younger or older worker. (Generational statements are, of course, generalizations, and each individual has his or her own preferences.)

The generations are broadly interdependent in a fast-changing workplace—older workers of the baby-boom cohort have institutional memory (which helps keep culture alive) and long experience in processes, so they can bring hard-won judgment and wisdom to a group's work at any level of authority. Generation X workers have seen and survived the great restructuring of work that has taken place in the last two decades; they are broadly adaptable, skeptical (in a good way), and self-reliant.

Millennial workers lead other generations in their adoption of new technology and new habits. Growing up online and in the new economy, they are more psychically footloose, less automatically loyal, and more prone to 24/7 connection. They have grown up with crowdsourcing opinion (think of Amazon star ratings) and the "expert amateurs" personified by bloggers. They are just as responsive as others are to appreciation and reward, however, and we have seen them adopt recognition solutions as quickly as they adopt other new technologies.

Roger Martin believes that millennial workers have a different relationship with work and money than previous generations. In 2014 he observed, "The current generation entering the workforce is more sensitive to the non-monetary, non-hierarchical benefits of their jobs than any prior generation of workers. They almost desperately want meaning in their work. As long as their employers think that they will be motivated first and foremost by incentive compensation or job promotions, there will continue to be big challenges in motivation and retention.

Employers need to focus more on creating a community that feels genuine to them and of which they feel an important part and less on designing compensation programs."[4]

However the next generation ("Generation Z") might differ in its tastes and attitudes, we believe that the trend toward multigenerational workforces is a long-term business reality. In fact, as baby boomers postpone retirement and businesses find it profitable to retain the boomers' experience with more flexible work arrangements, it's likely that by 2020 large organizations will find *four* distinct cultural generations working together. Business leaders who create a culture that unifies such disparate cohorts will harness an incredible range of knowledge, wisdom, and talent.

Recognition acts as a unifier in a multigenerational workplace because it crosses lines of authority, seniority, and social distance. A recognition moment confers respect and appreciation, which brings people together who might otherwise have a more remote workplace experience.

Research Insight

A Research Note by Aragon CEO Jim Lundy titled *Drive Employee Performance with Social Recognition* noted: "Social and corporate recognition need to be connected because doing so reinforces the right behaviors more effectively. By its nature, social recognition, which notifies the community when a manager or peer recognizes an associate, makes everyone aware of the recognition. Moreover, open-ended feedback and follow-up, available to and from everyone in the community, can extend and amplify the recognition, increasing its motivational value."[5]

Business Is Social

We are social beings, and our workplaces are small societies. The growth of social media shows the appeal of connection, but that need was hardwired into humans long before Facebook. From telling tales of our tribe around the fire 10,000 years ago to sharing pictures on Instagram, our biological imperative to bond and share changes expression but remains vital to who we are.

"Social business" means much more than social media. Work is interdependent, with all kinds of expertise needed at different stages of a project. Unlike the assembly line of 1915, though, projects are rarely linear treks from one task to another. Functions like product creation, customer service, marketing, financial management, and general management are all iterative processes—take an action, see what happens, and then choose another action. Entrepreneurial behavior is typically a series of efforts followed by feedback, which leads to new and different efforts.[6] Disciplines like customer response and financial management inform and change projects frequently.

People interact and need each other's interaction to succeed, and that requires social bonds like trust, communication, open-mindedness, respect, and appreciation to work well.

While the word *social* has become shorthand in business circles for "social networking technologies" like Facebook, Twitter, and LinkedIn (and many, many, more), we think the truly exciting development goes beyond technology to the habits and expectations that these technologies unleashed. Millennial employees are especially prone to share information of all kinds, but the habits are not by any means limited to personal information. Businesses use habits of instant messaging, cloud-based document sharing, quick feedback, and crowdsourcing information to make the most of everyone's brainpower. Creative conversation and problem solving are done at all times online, not just in a weekly meeting, and everyone from the newest entry-level employee to the far-flung distance worker to the senior executives can both join the conversation and witness it.

Breaking down social barriers is a good and necessary development of the interdependent workplace, and the breakdown is leading to some interesting new social standards.

For example, showing respect used to equate to showing deference. "Don't speak unless I ask you a question," was the command of the old-school manager. Now contributing—usefully and positively—is a sign of respect, and the effective manager solicits formal and informal suggestions (often on an internal company website).

As the workplace becomes more socially active in this sense, recognition reinforces the attitudes that facilitate cooperative work. We've spoken about the power of thanks to encourage engagement, and the benefits of sharing applause far and wide.

As social sharing becomes more and more a part of how work gets done, recognition can encourage all to contribute.

Leverage Social Sharing

Until the advent of "timelines" on social media, social sharing was an ephemeral phenomenon. Now people expect to relive social sharing over time by looking back at a record of messages, pictures, and videos they've shared. Similarly, as a system that records and analyzes recognition, social recognition creates a long-term narrative of social business behavior. As managers use recognition systems to visualize social sharing, heretofore hidden patterns emerge. For example, a map of the recognition moments among members of a department that works with great efficiency will reveal practices that lead to greater efficiency. Managers need not rely on anecdotal information of hazy memory but can pinpoint the moments and actions that lead to success.

Business Is Mobile

Another trend radically accelerated by technology is the recent shift toward mobile devices, chiefly smartphones and tablets. By mid-2013, even the world's largest PC maker, Lenovo, was selling more mobile devices than PCs.[7] And combined with cloud computing, even inexpensive mobile devices display incredible versatility and power.

China has more than 800 million smartphone users, India more than 300 million. Worldwide smartphone shipments in 2013 topped

1 billion units.[8] Smartphones are not "the platform of the future"—they are already today's global platform.

This is evident in the move to mobile devices for social networking. Social networking is an inherently mobile activity—spontaneous, unplanned, taking place whenever and wherever the impulse happens. More than 70 percent of U.S. consumers use mobile devices to access social media because they are a natural pairing.[9]

Social recognition among colleagues can—and should—be designed for use on mobile devices to increase participation. Employees should be able to share appreciation immediately, not waiting to get back to a desk, especially when that desk might be 1,000 miles away. A large portion of the global workforce is not chained to a computer all day. They are on the road, in the air, at the job site, on the floor. They don't have laptops around their necks. But you can bet a whole lot of them are carrying smartphones.

Ever more sophisticated software systems, including HR and talent management systems, are moving to a software as a service (SaaS) platform.[10] SaaS reverses the traditional enterprise computing model: Instead of a company buying and managing software with a large IT staff on site, another company manages certain applications and data remotely and delivers the capability instantly over the Internet in a web browser. (The experience feels just like using Google or Yahoo—all the computing happens remotely, but you see the result in your browser.) Salesforce .com was an early success story in SaaS, and services like Google Apps and Microsoft Office 365 are popular examples. SaaS software is updated automatically by the provider, which can also customize applications.

For social recognition, SaaS provides a lower-cost, more efficient, and more customizable system that can be integrated with other HR systems. A company's IT department doesn't have to worry about scalability—that is, adding servers and customizing capabilities as a company grows. In the spirit of global business, SaaS crosses geographical, monetary, and language barriers so a social recognition program can roll out to everyone in a company at once regardless of where they live or work. (And to be candid, HR is rarely the priority recipient of in-house technology resources. "Outsourcing" technological support by using SaaS means HR can implement a social recognition system without waiting until other departments' needs are filled by company IT staff.)

In addition to many financial and technological advantages of this model, SaaS puts tremendous computing power into inexpensive mobile devices through easy-to-use apps. For recognition, the result is a mobile "front end" that enables anyone at any time to recognize great work, and a powerful "back end" that captures the moment and manages the overall recognition program.

Two of recognition's best practices are *be accessible* and *be universal*. Mobile recognition does both, making recognition available to everyone, everywhere.

Mobile recognition needs to be integrated into the full system, not a stand-alone "eThanks" app. Mobile employees need the power to recognize and receive appreciation on the go, and their activity needs to feed into the social database. When that happens, the benefit of recognition translates fully to the fastest-growing technology.

Business Is Borrowing Consumer Technologies

The fifth movement to keep in mind is a response by business to employee habits: the "consumerizing" of business technology. Not long ago, business phones looked different from consumer phones. Business computer applications looked different from consumer applications. The business Internet was dominated by content for which people paid, and consumer content was "free" (actually, supported by advertising or Internet access fees).

Today, consumer-centric design dominates. The reason is related to the global, multigenerational, social, and mobile changes that are taking place: as the borderlines of time, space, and behavior between "work" and "life" break down, businesses are more open to adapting consumer technologies and habits to the workplace. As business applications work more like consumer applications, training time shortens and adoption rates rise. The business apps on your smartphone look and work a lot like your consumer apps.

At the leading edge of consumer-centric design, video recognition is a recent innovation, taking advantage of the broad move in how we absorb information from the written word to video messages. Businesses have had videoconferencing for more than a decade, but the technologies were expensive and somewhat artificial-feeling (think people in a conference room facing a camera). As broadband connections become ubiquitous and video calling appears in smartphones, we're seeing a new, less formal habit of communicating via video. When video recognition is built into your program, it's even easier for someone to create a quick but meaningful video containing the powerful specific messages of appreciation but delivered in an intimately personal way. Video naturally conveys tone of voice and body language along with our words of praise.

Business applications from sales activity records to financial analysis to marketing are undergoing a new generation of design in which text, video, audio, data visualization, and "infographics" are all working together in a single environment. The experience goes beyond getting data to finding meaning in the data instantly. Inspired by the combination of simplicity and richness of smartphones, and the power of SaaS and cloud technologies, we're in a new and incredibly diverse age of design in business.

Three additional consumer-oriented technologies in particular have influenced business thinking about recognition—24/7 connectedness, "free" rewards, and gamification. There are pros and cons to each trend.

24/7 Connectedness

"Working from home" once meant taking home a briefcase full of papers on the weekend. Now it means plugging into a cloud-based set of secure company applications and information with your tablet or smartphone. It means greater flexibility and productivity by removing barriers of time and space. Jason Averbook, author of *HR from Now to Next*, calls this *enabling people to work, the way they work, outside of work*.

It also means new questions about what constitutes a workday. If I save two hours of commuting time because the company provides technology for me to work remotely, does that time belong to the company or to me? If the company asks me to review a report at 10:00 a.m. on a Saturday, can I do my personal e-mail on Monday? Is my habit of 24/7 connectedness to my Twitter feeds beneficial to the company because half of the tweets I read are relevant to work? The answers to these questions and dozens more are sometimes found in formal company policies and sometimes as informal standards—and often just as adapted behaviors (as in, "Honey, please don't read your work e-mails at the dinner table.").

This 24/7 connectedness leads to an alternative view of life-work balance called *life-work blending*, in which both realms recognize the other's importance and need to cooperate when it comes to time and focus. As management consultant and author Ron Ashkenas wrote in *Forbes*, we need to become flexible in how we accomplish both our work goals and our personal goals.[11] Both need to recognize the other's importance.

Recognition's emphasis on human emotions, motivations, and personal connection in a business context fits philosophically with this view.

In recognition, the time shift to 24/7 connectedness is similar to the location shift of mobile computing. It improves program adoption by removing barriers to use. There may not be time in a day to recognize a colleague, but later, recalling her good job, I should be able to easily nominate her for an award. And the benefit is twofold, because she might first learn of that award outside of office hours. If 24/7 connectedness means life-work blending, shouldn't the benefits and good news reach employees just as easily as demands?

"Free" Recognition A.K.A. Badging

Some recognition systems promise "free" recognition in the form of online badges or "thumbs-up" icons. They borrow the notion from popular features of social networks such as Facebook's "like" icon. HR people have gone so far as to tell us that they like the feature precisely because it's free (and they believe the benefit is implicit).

Let's step back a moment and realize that these are just techniques, recently arrived, that are popular both because they indicate an emotion and because they are very easy to give. They are practically effortless, and therein lies their potential to defeat the purpose of a recognition practice.

Whether recognition is given by a peer or a manager, there needs to be a scale of the level of recognition that is reflective of the level of achievement. Without differentiation, recognition loses its relevance.

Tom might get a "thumbs-up" from Sarah because he helped her straighten out a $100 discrepancy in a payment. When Nigella saves half a million dollars for the company as a consequence of spotting a critical quality error in a product, should she also get a "thumbs-up"? These are both actions worthy of appreciation; one is clearly more valuable than the other, and the reward should be appropriate to the scale of the achievement. The trick is not to devalue the power of thanks through inappropriate recognition not commensurate with the level of effort or result achieved.

Let's say an employee nominates many people for awards. She's on the alert for good work, as she's putting in voluntary effort to recognize others. If she had an incentive beyond her voluntary participation (such as a badge for "top nominator"), then the data becomes skewed. Recognition suddenly becomes unnatural; the artificial stimulus makes ensuing awards less sincere and legitimate. This can poison a recognition program. It's critical for employees and managers to be inspired by the great work itself, not the promise of badges or personal awards for the nominating.

What You Can Learn from a Dinner Party

We have a saying about recognition: "If it has no value, it has no value." To illustrate, imagine you come to a small dinner party.

Scenario one: You arrive with absolutely nothing in your hands, sit, and start eating the dinner. Dinner is lovely, and at the end of the dinner, you take out a piece of paper, draw a big thumbs-up on it, hand it to your host, and say, "This was a magical dinner, I really like your dinner. I'm gonna like you on Facebook! Heck, this dinner was so good I'm going to give you a second thumbs-up!" That's like badging.

Scenario two: You say, "That was a really fabulous dinner; you must have spent a lot of money in putting this together. Let me get my wallet out, I want to contribute for how much . . . Here's $50 for what I ate." That's like recognizing with cash.

Scenario three: You arrive with a bottle of wine, chocolates, or flowers, or you offer to bring a special dessert, which amounts to coming prepared to show appreciation. And perhaps after the event you send a handwritten note or an entertaining e-card, and yes, you *also* post a photo on Facebook!

Badging, cash, or giving a considered sign of appreciation—which makes the best impression?

Gamification

Gamification is a hot trend in program design, showing up in how we spend our leisure time, how we buy, and most recently, how we work. The term *gamification* means adding elements of game design or game mechanics to nongame contexts. In the workplace, it could include elements like awarding points for hitting milestones and competing for prizes.

While businesspeople have long been fond of comparing corporate strategy to chess, or contract negotiations to poker, we're talking about the stimulus-response design of video games, computer games, and especially online games. People play these on mobile phones and tablets; rewards are earned for attaining new "levels" of achievement, colorful graphics abound, and often a crowd of fellow gamers connects online. Video games are fun, addictive, and wildly popular.

Gamification is a serious subject for neuroscientists, educators, and designers of everything from software to robots to business processes. Gaming is fundamentally a "feedback loop" of actions and responses, including progress monitoring and rewards. Since a sense of making progress is fundamental to engagement,[12] adding game elements to work can inspire greater engagement. Companies consider gamification in recognition programs to motivate and engage employees, and to increase participation.

What many people call gamification—points, badges, titles—can mask the expert design that makes games such powerful motivators. It is imperative to understand gamification—and what makes it work—before jumping in. In recognition, game design must connect achievement to company goals and values. For example, if game design encourages competition for badges or points on a leaderboard in a zero-sum environment (I win, you lose), it actively discourages teamwork.

Gamification is ideal for making some tasks more appealing by inserting a competitive or a fun, game-like element. It also may be useful in HR programs, such as learning, where participation levels are low. Another example of where gamification makes sense is in a sales contest. In a sales contest, you want immediate and broad participation as well as competitive behavior. Competitive environments are often the lifeblood for effective sales programs. This differs from a recognition program, as you don't need—or want—an artificial stimulus in a recognition program as it's something people want to naturally do!

Here are four myths about gamification that separate the good from the bad:

Myth #1: Gamification Means Awarding Points

Gamification can be unpacked into two different qualities, both found in gaming environments. One, which experts call *pointsification*, includes things like status icons, scoreboards, and badges. The other, which experts call *ludification* (or playfulness)[13] is achievement-based and includes elements like skill-based learning and "big wins" that come from achieving something difficult, unexpected, or arduous. Ludification makes games appealing (and addictive). Yes, gamification can be built on points, extrinsic motivation, and transactional engagement. But good gamification concentrates far more on ludification, intrinsic motivators, and emotional engagement. That means a recognition solution can take advantage of game design without ever offering a point, badge, or status icon.

Myth #2: Gamification Makes Any Process Better

Gamification certainly has many benefits. When done well it can increase production, build teamwork, and motivate employees to achieve goals, create fun and enjoyment, inspire friendly competition, and increase voluntary engagement. But when gamification is implemented in a haphazard way or onto the wrong processes—or focused only on pointsification—there is danger of:

- Goals shifting to "winning" when winning isn't what's important
- Cheating or "gaming" the system
- Keeping thinking "inside the box"
- Masking a flawed product or process
- A need for constantly rising stakes to preserve engagement

Introducing artificial stimuli into a process can distort the connection between reward and outcome. The moment the "game" becomes more important than the behaviors and values that deserve recognition, the practice becomes self-defeating.

Myth #3: Gamification Creates Motivation

Gamification almost always provides some sort of motivation. But not all motivation is equal. As we saw in Chapter 5, motivation can be extrinsic or intrinsic. When game design requires an ever-escalating set of external rewards, it's feeding extrinsic motivation. Successful gamification, like the successful use of rewards discussed in Chapter 5, feeds intrinsic motivation by stimulating feelings of achievement, mastery, or approval. For this reason, a recognition system that "rewards the rewarders" runs the risk of encouraging people to nominate others for their own reward, which distorts the central motivation for giving recognition.[14]

Intrinsic motivation is self-propagating and more powerful as part of social recognition. Rather than try to "create" motivation with gamification, a social recognition system should identify, reward, and celebrate that motivation that comes from within.

Myth #4: Gamification Creates Engagement

Games are engaging in the sense that they stimulate extra effort, but like motivation, engagement has two flavors: transactional engagement and emotional engagement. Here are differences between the two forms of engagement in a business context:

Transactional Engagement	Emotional Engagement
▪ Pay for performance	▪ Attached to work and company
▪ Does what is required as long as rewards are forthcoming	▪ Desire to do more and get more in return
▪ More likely to jump ship for a better offer	▪ More likely to stay the course

The wrong game design stimulates transactional engagement only and never becomes self-sustaining.

There are business situations in which gamification is a clear benefit. In a sales contest, for example, you want immediacy, energy, and competitive behavior among leaders on a leaderboard. Sales representatives are natural scorekeepers. But not every business situation calls for internal competition.

Gamification in recognition must answer the specific tenets of recognition that we've discussed such as tying behavior to company values, expressing authentic appreciation, and conferring appropriate awards. It holds promise for such recognition activities as learning a new skill or completing baseline activities like creating a public profile, and thus it has a place when correctly deployed. Be sure your solution taps into the right motivators and the right sort of engagement for maximum effectiveness.

Technology Refocuses on Human Nature

When we talk about social recognition, we want people to focus back on the fundamental reality of what truly motivates people, what has the power to inspire sustainable success and growth.

Modern business adapts quickly to change. It recognizes change in society and leverages change to further its vision and mission. In the best case, business leads employees to a new way of working that returns to the basic human truths, cutting out layers of fear or bureaucracy that hinder engagement, inspiration, and loyalty.

All the movements we've discussed—global, multigenerational, social, mobile and consumer-driven—are enabled by new technology, but they are fundamentally in service of human needs to connect, work, and live in such a way that all employees can be proud to participate in something bigger than themselves.

That's the power of thanks. In the next chapter, we'll share the best ways to bring this power into your workplace.

PART 3
PUTTING SOCIAL RECOGNITION INTO PRACTICE

7 | Building a Social Recognition Framework

The global engineering and construction company Bechtel does big projects. Big, as in putting out 650 oil field fires in Kuwait after the 1991 war, and big, as in building Britain's high-speed Channel Tunnel Rail Link. Bechtel's 53,000 employees manage projects of mind-boggling complexity for their customers, and they manage their internal practices with similar attention to process and detail. "We specialize in big complex projects—the more complex the better," says Susan McCullough, Bechtel's Global Manager of Compensation and Benefits.

And Leader+, Bechtel's recognition program, is unapologetically detailed, incorporating no fewer than 18 values that represent Bechtel's Leadership Model. "We had a global implementation," says McCullough. "We started out thinking this would be good for the non-exempt population, to get them motivated throughout the year. As we looked at the power of the [recognition] tool, we said, 'let's do it for everyone . . . right up to the executive level.'" With 34 different currencies to manage, in 140 countries, Bechtel's single central budget for recognition is carefully monitored and tracked.

"We're a very traditional company," says McCullough. "We used to have a very structured approval authority—it took supervisors as well as the head of HR in one of our businesses to approve any award. [Now] peer-to-peer recognition is a big piece of what we have implemented. We want to reflect a culture of recognition and have the culture of recognition be consistent across the whole organization."

McCullough's implementation stresses the need to publicize social recognition. She says, "I had senior management in different businesses calling me and saying, 'we want to do more with Leader+. How can you help us advertise this and get it out in front of our employees?' Now, it's no longer corporate-driven. All levels of employees are taking the initiative to communicate it."

*   *   *

Building a core company culture is like nurturing a bonsai tree. It takes a lot of time and energy to get your core company culture going in the right way. If you cut down your bonsai tree, it will take you an awfully long time to grow another one. A bonsai tree might seem worlds away from creating a culture, but the process of growing, nurturing, and sustaining both requires similar care.

The recognition journey takes on a new momentum when you commit to a social recognition strategy. It is a defined practice with clear implementation steps, all meant to grow and nurture that bonsai tree. It takes time and energy and resources to implement, and once in place, it protects and nurtures your culture.

If an investor asked, "What is your compensation strategy?" you'd drop on the desk a three-ring binder filled with everything having to do with compensation: base pay, salary bands, grades, bonuses—all of it. If the investor then asked, "Explain your talent strategy," you'd have three-ring binders stuffed with information about 401(k)s, health and education benefits, savings plans, profit sharing, and stock options for employees. You'd have a plan for continuous improvement of your website's "Careers" section, a modern social recruiting strategy, and a list of high-potential employees. You'd tell the investor about training and succession planning.

Next the investor asks, "What's your strategic plan?" You roll out a 60-slide deck filled with product plans, customer profiles, marketing plans, and financial performance data.

This strategic thinking is a hallmark of a growing, smart company—a set of plans and practices that will advance your mission and growth in the coming years.

When we ask executives, "Tell me about your recognition strategy," however, they often have no binder, no deck of slides, no metrics, and no execution plan. They might be on a recognition journey to the extent that they have a tactical or enterprise recognition program, but compare that to all the practices named above! Recognition is typically not treated as a strategic priority. Recognition, for all its importance, is often an outlier, not subject to the same rigorous planning and monitoring as other management practices.

Recognition can and should be planned and executed in a company like any other management practice with the potential to drive bottom-line results, and therein lies the opportunity for competitive advantage. Other practices like compensation, financial discipline, and quality control are so well established that your competition manages these in essentially the same way as you. When you elevate recognition to the level of other strategic practices, you create a fresh competitive advantage, one that is uniquely tailored to your company's culture, goals, and strategy. Social recognition is one of the few practices that still create competitive advantage.

This chapter is a blueprint for building a strategically effective social recognition practice that seizes that competitive advantage. This blueprint includes plans in five areas: sponsorship, design, reach, adoption, and rewards (Figure 7.1).

Sponsorship

The success of a strategic recognition program depends on sponsorship by organization leaders.

The Tempo Starts at the Top

Contrast the following scenarios.

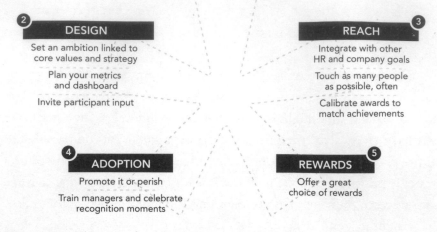
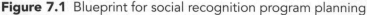

Figure 7.1 Blueprint for social recognition program planning

Scenario A: Like most of your competitors, you give all responsibility for a recognition program to "Bob and Mary," midlevel workers in the HR department. Bob and Mary, the recognition program managers, are low on the chain of command. They have no business planning experience. They don't understand how you develop a strategy in a company. They're told to get a recognition program going, but they are neither equipped nor required to operate recognition as a strategic practice.

Instead their program and budget suits a nice-to-have perk for the rank-and-file. An incentive company sales representative asks them, "Well, what's your budget? We'll help you spend that budget." The incentive company encourages Bob and Mary to put all their money into exciting, colorful posters, entertaining training for managers, and merchandise. The incentive-company rep gives Bob and Mary a catalog of reward items and encourages employees to select from what the incentive company has in its warehouse.

When you talk to the company's C-level executives about recognition, they say, "Oh, yeah, I think we have a program. That's Bob and Mary's job, right?"

Scenario B: Bob and Mary, experienced HR managers, present a social recognition program at a meeting of all top executives, including their boss, the head of HR. This group constitutes a green-light committee for every strategic corporate initiative. Bob and Mary demonstrate the costs and benefits of a social recognition program in hard financial terms. They go on to describe intangible benefits of the program, again showing real-world projections for outcomes like increased engagement and lower turnover, and point out that these intangible benefits produce tangible results. They cite Towers Watson's finding that a 15 percent improvement in employee engagement correlates with a 2 percent improvement in operating margin[1] and Aon Hewitt's study showing that every percentage point increase in employee engagement drives 0.6 percent growth in sales.[2] Their summary slide shows the one- and three-year returns on investment for the recognition program.

> *A 15 percent improvement in engagement drives a 2 percent improvement in operating margin.*

Now when you ask the C-level executives about recognition, they say, "We have a recognition program; it's part of our strategic talent plan, and Bob and Mary report monthly on progress toward their ROI goal, like everyone else."

In Scenario B, recognition is structured and run as a strategic initiative, delivering competitive advantage (from outcomes like increased engagement) and savings (from outcomes like lower turnover) to the corporate bottom line.

As a strategic initiative, Scenario B also requires executive support. When recognition's relationship to other strategic assets is understood and supported, its power is truly unleashed, and this can only happen with executive attention and approval. Social recognition earns support because it engages executives where they live—in the realms of competitive advantage, high performance, and profits.

Social recognition needs commitment from all top executives. It's one challenge to get a budget granted, and another to command the attention and time of busy leaders in implementing a recognition program. This might not seem logical—after all, what's worth spending money on is worth supporting—but nonetheless it's possible to see social recognition crowded out by other strategic programs. We believe *executive participation* elevates the program to strategic status. It increases general participation, focuses managers, and battles the unfortunate tendency to say yes without real commitment.

Commitment also means applying resources like financial management, program management, marketing, and compliance with different legal and tax regulations. These should be sourced from elsewhere within the company if the HR department doesn't have the expertise. Work with department heads to estimate the scale of resource required and build it into your recognition plan before you present it to executive management.

Leaders at different levels of the organization all have their own roles in a successful program.

Senior Executive Sponsor(s)—the Global Program "Champions"

For greatest program impact, one or more executive sponsors must be accountable for delivering all of the program's components in accordance with the vision. They must agree to monitor and discuss the quarterly executive dashboard and take action to guarantee the program moves forward like any product initiative. The company's head of HR at the very least should be an executive sponsor. Ideally the CEO or business unit presidents will be directly involved, too.

Executive sponsors:

- Drive global program awareness at a senior level
- Sign off on program design and implementation
- Validate global program goals
- Support the program's implementation over time

Finally, executive sponsors should have a personal presence in your communications. If you send out a monthly e-mail listing those who have been recognized that month, it should go out with the signature of an executive sponsor. A personal communication from an executive to an award winner has a huge impact on the winner and on the program's reputation.

In-House Program Manager(s)

Whether this is Bob and Mary in HR or the senior director of operations, this person has ultimate accountability for designing the program and launching it to greatest effect. This is also the main contact with any outside vendors and the person who chooses what models to follow.

Program managers:

- Define goals, objectives, criteria, processes, benchmarks, and measurements of success
- Drive company-wide consistency and equity of rewards
- Drive the program globally (in a large firm)

Local or Departmental Program "Champions"

Program champions, as symbols of executive support, are critical for two reasons. First, if members of the executive team are divided on the importance of recognition, there's a distinct possibility of neglect or a benign brand of sabotage—the death of many initiatives. Second, local champions are the experts when it comes to resolving cultural differences, such as equity in award levels or traditions for recognizing and rewarding behavior. Champions provide strategic and tactical vision as well, which speeds the success of the program.

Program champions:

- Position the global initiative locally (internal marketing)
- Drive program goals and objectives locally
- Provide local validation of global program goals (big picture)
- Mediate challenges resulting from proposed local changes to achieve global consistency

In any configuration, executive support helps prevent the classic problem of "push versus pull," that is, the tendency of executives to launch a program "push" with great fanfare by pushing messages and promoting the program in meetings and through other venues. This is well and good, but the "pull" of seeing executives actually participating in recognition, going on the project teams, helping design the rewards, congratulating recognition on the awards social feed, and walking the talk speaks far more strongly about the program's importance.

Expert Insight

"Before investing in social recognition, reward and performance technologies, ensure the culture of the organization is ready for such processes. In cultures where social performance processes thrive, command-and-control hierarchies give way to more network-style organizations, and social recognition and rewards become daily examples of employees living the brand and core values of the organization."

—Yvette Cameron, Research Director,
*Gartner Predicts 2014: Nexus Forces ·
Redefine Human Capital Management*[3]

Design

Recognition must be designed as carefully as any other strategic initiative, with a clear ambition, metrics and input from stakeholders.

Set an Ambition Linked to Core Values and Strategy

Why are you doing this? Without real, detailed goals, the practice of engaging and motivating employees can become "recognition for recognition's sake," which typically results in another old-school program lacking accountability and relevance.

Establish a recognition ambition based on your organization's core values and strategic objectives. What are the hallmarks of your culture? What do you want to accomplish? How does it relate to your most important business drivers? What must be supported—profits, customer service, operational excellence, innovation, and/or maximum product quality?

Often the goal of a recognition program begins with the question, "What is missing that would move our strategy ahead?" For example, do you want to increase employee engagement? If so, you need to increase both the commitment of employees to their work *and* their alignment with company goals. Commitment without alignment means wasted effort (and frustration). Alignment without commitment means wasted potential (and employee turnover). Recognition singles out great performance (commitment) that focuses on strategic goals (alignment).

A survey of companies by WorldatWork in 2013 found these to be the most frequently cited goals for recognition programs (Figure 7.2).[4]

What are the objectives/goals of your organization's recognition programs?

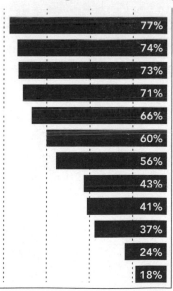

Percentage	Objective/Goal
77%	Recognize years of service
74%	Create positive work environment
73%	Create culture of recognition
71%	Motivate high performance
66%	Reinforce desired behaviors
60%	Increase morale
56%	Support mission/values
43%	Encourage loyalty
41%	Increase retention
37%	Being an employer of choice
24%	Line of sight to company goals
18%	Support culture of change

Figure 7.2 The most frequently cited goals for recognition programs

Whatever your strategic goals, they must be written down, so you can focus supporting programs and objectives through the lens of your strategic goals. Here's an example from Intuit:

Intuit's Recognition Ambition

Drive higher employee engagement at Intuit.

Improve employee satisfaction survey results.

Create a culture of recognition throughout Intuit.

Continue to make Intuit a "Best Place to Work."

Each of Intuit's goals can be affirmed over time—does employee engagement improve (as measured by surveys such as the Gallup Q12 or Towers Watson models)? What do employee satisfaction surveys tell over time? Are line managers able to observe and describe changes in both commitment and alignment? That's focus.

Hotel group IHG manages to place two of its key branding terms—"BrandHearted" employees and "Great Hotels Guests Love"—into its recognition ambition. Here it is (in the British spelling IHG uses for its global programs):

IHG's Recognition Objectives

- Support IHG corporate and reservations centres employees in recognising BrandHearted colleagues
- Uphold a culture where people love to come to work
- Make global recognition easy
- Motivate and engage colleagues by demonstrating that those who go the extra mile in creating Great Hotels Guests Love are recognised and rewarded, which in turn encourages others to do the same

Ambitions may also be stated as strategic goals for the recognition program, as in this example from Symantec:

Strategic Goals for Recognition at Symantec

All recognition programs globally will be migrated to one platform, with one common brand and one executive dashboard

One global recognition solution

Drive employee loyalty

Reward behaviors that support company values

Local impact and relevance for all employees globally

These are some of the most common goals; yours must be specific to your organization's ambitions, market position, and challenges. Take time to define these goals clearly, for without them, recognition will not be taken seriously as a strategic initiative. (Without clear goals, moreover, you'll be tempted to judge your program's effectiveness by anecdote or gut feel. This almost guarantees mediocrity.)

State goals as direct outcomes, even if factors beyond recognition come into play. For example, human resources professionals know that recognition can contribute to employee retention even though other factors such as retention bonuses, company culture, and personal ambitions also come into play. In such cases, shared goals can be considered against joint outcomes by tracking all relevant efforts. (Similar to the way that saving costs and increasing revenue contribute together to higher profits.)

Clear goals are critical when starting a program. We often say that, because recognition isn't taught in management school, most managers are ill equipped to make use of it. More often than not, managers avoid a new practice like recognition that requires time and training to learn. That's why they need goals. Measurement against goals helps to ensure that recognition receives appropriate priority in a busy manager's schedule.

Naming your program ambitions in detail also informs program design. Factors such as the adaptability of your line managers can play a significant role in the effectiveness of recognition, and ambitions help you consider these factors. Early in your design of a recognition program, ask the questions that set a size and scope for your efforts, such as:

- How aggressive do we want to be? (e.g., how soon do we hit goal A? How soon do we hit goal B?)
- What resources do we need to start and continue the program?
- How fast can our managers learn this new skill?
- What other programs are in the pipeline at this time?
- Which departments (e.g., training, communications, finance) need to be involved in ongoing operation of the program?
- How do we report progress?
- What is the best rollout path?

Answering these questions in detail early on means a more cost-effective and powerful program later.

Consider your organization's values in the context we've discussed earlier—what does your company choose when you must allocate resources or prioritize outcomes? You might say this goes beyond a "statement of values," which is about an organization's identity, to an "application of values," which is about how that identity is applied day to day.

Here are a few value-specific criteria for recognition to help you choose. Try choosing the top three.

These are not either-or trade-offs, but the value of choosing just three is to guide choices you will make as you advance, for example balancing time and cost choices early to best achieve your aims.

Once you've identified the top three value criteria for your program, make sure that everything you do drives toward these goals. It will keep you focused, and it will help ensure your success.

Prioritize Your Vision and Values

___ I want to emotionally engage my employees with the company.

___ I want to ensure our corporate values are understood by all employees.

___ I want to enable my employees to overcome roadblocks and frustration.

___ I want to see the vast majority of my employees touched by recognition.

___ I want to encourage people at all levels to recognize their coworkers.

___ I want to encourage communication and relationships among my employees.

___ I want to improve my business and financial results.

___ I want to unify a diverse set of cultures into one.

___ I want a universal, global, and equitable reward program.

___ I want to improve employee happiness and reduce turnover.

___ I want to ensure compliance with internal and external regulations.

___ I want to keep costs under control.

___ I want to consolidate multiple programs.

___ I want all recognition rewards to be compliant with tax codes.

___ I want deeper insight into my culture and values.

___ I want deeper insight into my employees and their performance.

___ I want data that will let me better manage or drive change.

Plan Your Metrics and Dashboard

Business planning concludes with accountability. Whose budget gets spent, and who gets the benefits counted against his or her end-of-year review? Who will see to it that each component of the program is accomplished? Accountability is about doing what you say, standing by your planning, and being open about amending your plan as you go. It means quarterly executive reporting (at least that often), real-time activity reporting for managers, and openness about progress. It also means holding vendors accountable for the standards of your program.

Once you have clear goals, translate those ambitions into measurable achievements to make recognition meaningful to executive leadership. Recognition metrics should reflect what's important in the corporate culture based on its values. Metrics should also relate directly to the actions that further your strategic goals, such as improved productivity, cost containment, and employee retention.

1. Show how certain recognition behaviors drive employee performance (which also identifies best practices within your culture).
2. Link recognition to the organization's financial statements and corporate goals.

A number of metrics should be monitored to judge the effectiveness of your recognition program. They include:

- 80 to 90+ percent of employees touched by the program (as nominators or recipients)
- More than 60 percent of employees are regular participants, nominating others or receiving recognition at least six times a year
- A six-month survey shows 90 percent of managers participating
- A one-year survey confirms that 90 percent of employees agree "the program helps motivate sustained high performance"
- Program reaches all geographic and demographic groups of the organization
- Award distribution matches performance bell curve (see next section)
- Award frequency met by managers within six months of training
- One unified system meets budgetary goals at six- and twelve-month milestones
- A two-year internal company survey shows a double-digit increase in employee engagement
- Company values are selected as award reasons by division, region, or business line, as appropriate

Measurement means relevance. Without it, any project tends to justify itself. The lonely corners of companies are cluttered with once-promising initiatives that lacked measures of success or failure. Often in recognition programs, standards of success are applied later in the game, simply to legitimize the project, instead of at the outset; this makes the metrics at best suspicious and at worst irrelevant.

The bottom line is, if you don't know what you're working toward before you begin, how will you know when you've arrived?

Determine your metrics *before* execution begins, then faithfully report against those metrics on a regular schedule, even if the outcome isn't what you hoped. Negative results can be the most valuable, as they show you the areas where you most need to improve. In companies where such failure is permitted, continual improvement is possible, not just in a recognition program but across the board.

If your organization has project managers, use their tools (or better yet, get a project manager on the recognition team) to keep the setup and execution on schedule for a smooth program launch. Then use periodic surveys to measure such factors as the ones described above.

Identify recognition opportunities as you implement the program. Use the power of thanks to reinforce managers who understand and embrace the program, who realize improvements in their staff as the program continues, and who encourage and teach recognition as mentors to other managers. In other words, make progress in recognition important enough to recognize and reward!

With metrics established, an effective social recognition program requires a way for managers to track the program's progress (just as managers must track budgets). This is best done at the manager level, using the concept of a "dashboard" that displays recognition activity of all kinds.

Actual performance dashboards for managers create accountability. If your organization is already using a dashboard system, it's a good idea to adapt that format to a recognition program. (This helps the adoption rate for a new program.) A dashboard report should be defined with the company-wide strategic metrics at the top as well as departmental key performance indicators (KPIs). KPIs include overall penetration levels, penetration of each division/department, and operational necessities such as award approval/disapproval levels, enterprise budget targets, and similar data.

> *Performance dashboards for managers create accountability.*

Tracking a large number of recognition awards gives greater relevance to the dashboards because they render broader data across the company and along the bell curve of employees. All of this information is made more accurate, and more actionable, by high penetration of the recognition program. Capture the data from a program with 80 to 90 percent participation, and you'll have a deep, dynamic view of how the company culture is driving results. An elitist recognition program, with 5 to 10 percent penetration, is statistically unreliable (if only the top innovators are recognized for innovation, how can you know if innovation is on everyone's mind?). The manager's dashboard is a gateway to this greater insight. Globally, the aggregate analysis of many awards, their causes and effects, creates a nuanced and detailed look at employee engagement, productivity, and morale.

At an operational level, program metrics such as number of awards per department must be broken down into relevant targets for each division, department, or country leader. These leaders will have their individual activity metrics communicated to them via "push" mechanisms as well as always-available real-time "pull" reports and will be accountable for monitoring their progress. Ideally this will be included in the MBO (management by objectives) plans for these managers. By setting penetration levels of recognition in their departments, reviewing recognition metrics regularly, and tweaking the program as necessary, the social recognition program will naturally become part of the management rhythm.

Why set a target? Because a target confirms the importance of a social recognition program and the validity of its goals and, like a budget target, enables managers to track progress on the way to their goals—and helps make them accountable for meeting those goals.

Granting recognition awards in the moment for behaviors demonstrated (or authorizing them, when the manager's role is approving another person's award) is different from awarding a sales bonus, which is a pre-planned performance incentive based on achieving a predetermined goal. Also, unlike a sales quota or incentive program, social recognition is given as small awards in an organic and spontaneous manner by many members of the company, and thus they are enlisted in making the program work. The manager is accountable for demonstrating the value of social recognition to his or her staff.

Combined with the metrics that monitor social recognition activity on an enterprise level, the data on social recognition updates continuously, and the program manager can spot where recognition is not happening, which encourages accountability. For that matter, the program manager can also spot the excellent practitioners of recognition (both giving and receiving) and celebrate them early, often, and publicly. That's positive reinforcement for all.

These metrics are diagnostic and carry a powerful message that executive management cares about the program. Reports should go up the organization, ideally all the way to the CEO. This causes a cascade effect down the line; when everybody from the top down has a stake in hitting the goals, the clarity, urgency, and importance of the program magnifies. Everyone with authority is responsible, and the cascade of participation spreads learning through informal networks and through their relationships with managers (there's the social architecture at work again).

When you integrate these metrics into your systems of performance management, compensation, and reward, social recognition takes its deserved place alongside other MBO objectives.

Invite Participant Input

A program that improves employee alignment and commitment needs input from a cross-section of employee leaders, from high-ranking executives to hourly workers. Individuals ultimately implement culture change, and so gathering input from all levels early is helpful. The owner of the recognition program will do this informally or systematically (such as surveying a random sampling of employees or conducting focus groups) according to the organization's traditions.

As you clarify your vision for recognition, balance the need for broad input against the need for a process that moves forward. We've seen different companies implement this differently. For example, an advisory board made up of employees, managers, and executives can provide early suggestions that higher-ups might miss. Middle managers and line employees are especially aware of the invisible but powerful social architecture of your organization, which is a necessary component of cultural change.

That's not the same as designing a recognition program by polling, however. The common theme in successful program design is that the program owners ultimately have authority to move ahead. If everyone you survey has a vote (or veto) you'll never get out of the visioning phase. Best practices suggest that you solicit input early, show and explain your decisions along the way, and reinforce the principles you are following in your communication. For example, if you poll employees on what they want for rewards, they will always reply, "cash," and expect it. If, on the other hand, you first communicate to leaders and employees in general why a noncash system is preferable, you can enlist support at launch, rather than risking nonparticipation because people feel they haven't been heard or had a chance to consider the reasoning behind your decisions.

Keep the conversation focused on your core values: Why do employees support the company's overall mission? Hear in their words what motivates them, and who is most engaged and effective. You might survey employees to establish benchmarks in employee sentiment. If your organization is large or diversified, enlist helpers across divisions. If your organization is global, it is essential to get recommendations from locally based employees on such matters as local culture and preferred style of recognition. These early participants can become advocates and mentors to the larger company as you roll out the program.

Reach

Social recognition ideally touches everyone in the company, because it is most effective when everyone participates. Moreover, the psychological benefits of appreciation are good for anyone, whatever their role, seniority or position in the hierarchy.

Integrate Recognition with HR and Company Goals

As part of the everyday life of the company, social recognition needs to answer to the business goals of the company and the specific goals of HR. This means modeling a process throughout the organization, where hundreds or thousands of recognition moments are recorded, tracked, and measured.

A business case for recognition shows the cost of the program and its expected benefits. Your organization will have a preferred form of business case, and we recommend using that template to the greatest extent possible. At least calculate the true monetary cost of the problems a recognition program helps to fix (low productivity, high turnover, disengagement) and the benefits it inspires (increased sales, greater quality, a safer work environment, and improved customer service).

Here's a simple example of a business benefit—decreasing employee turnover. Lack of recognition for a job well done is the second most common reason people quit (after compensation). Employees who report on surveys that they are not adequately recognized at work are three times as likely to quit in the next 12 months. The 48.3 percent of voluntary departures that cite lack of recognition represent a preventable turnover cost. (See the turnover cost calculator in Chapter 8.)[5]

You can perform similar planning on top-line factors such as improving market penetration rates and quality, for example, if you can measure how quality increases lead to greater market penetration and thus, revenue.

In addition to a business case for recognition, securing executive support requires advance strategic assessment and planning. Earlier chapters described the nature of social recognition and its power to build company culture. The action steps outlined in this chapter are a practical framework for assessing, planning, and implementing social recognition as a long-term strategic practice in your organization.

Just the process of planning a social recognition program might change your perspective. For example, you might initially state, "The goal of our recognition program is to clean up our years-of-service awards program." That's a good goal, but as you go through the process you might see it as more a tactical element of a recognition program than a strategic business goal you can reach through social recognition.

Social recognition requires sufficient budgeting, and our work with leading corporations as well as authoritative studies such as those by WorldatWork's *Trends in Employee Recognition* put that figure at 1 to 2 percent of payroll.[6] Now, we can hear you say, "Whoa, we don't have 1 to 2 percent of payroll set aside. How are we going to do that?" The solution, once again, is found in treating the social recognition program as an investment.

First, you will not achieve the program's goals if the program is not appropriately resourced. One of the failings of old-style recognition is its implication that all recognition programs are more or less the same. That's like saying, "Let's buy the cheapest payroll system because they're all alike." Recognition programs, like payroll systems or any other enabling technology, have to justify their cost based on the value they generate, which is the point of modeling and measuring.

Like any enabling technology, however, social recognition bears a flexible series of costs—more so than most, in fact, because the monetary value of recognition awards covers a wide range. The practice can be instituted incrementally. Going from 0 to 1 percent in one year can be difficult, and so some companies start with a budget of 0.5 percent of payroll for their recognition program, and then increase by 0.1 or 0.15 percent per year. It can also become budget-neutral as part of a total rewards strategy. In a nonrecessionary year companies typically allocate 3 percent of the payroll budget for merit increases. If you rethink your annual bonus into recognition given throughout the year, you can get much greater return for your investment in "bonus." So as part of a total rewards strategy, you might reallocate 0.25 percent from the merit increase to the recognition program.

Indeed, some companies achieve 1 percent of payroll for recognition budget immediately by reallocating funds from the annual bonus pool. This practice is a logical extension of the rationale for bonuses. Think of it as the bonus spend working all year long instead of one time a year, with incremental rewards and appreciation for exactly the results you hope a bonus program will achieve.

Incidentally, many large companies are already spending 1 to 2 percent or more of payroll in ad hoc recognition programs; they just don't recognize it as such. Those well-intentioned, informal acts of recognition taking the department out for dinner, or buying tickets to the ball game as a thank-you—tend to be obscured as expenses in travel and entertainment budgets. We've known CFOs who have tried to separate these expenses to discover what informal recognition costs, and they never get to the bottom of it. More concerning, these ad hoc recognition moments funded through expense reports are not appropriately taxed, opening the company to risk.

MYTHBUSTER
Preallocation of points is best

When thinking about recognition program design and funding, some program managers think it easiest to simply designate a certain number of points to each program participant on a monthly or quarterly basis. Participants are then responsible for distributing these points on a "use it or lose it" basis. The challenge with this approach is twofold:

1. The emphasis is improperly assigned to the giving of points and not to the behaviors, achievements, contributions, or results worthy of recognition. People become consumed with "points" and not with great effort deserving of praise. With points burning a hole in their pocket, some nominators will look for anything to recognize, not the truly important, relevant, or game-changing.

2. People tend to hoard points at the beginning of a period, worried they will run out and not be able to reward an above-and-beyond effort at the end of the period. ("I just saw Susan demonstrate terrific customer service, but it's only the beginning of the month. What if Julie or Tom does something even better at the end of the month? I'd better wait and see what happens.") Then, when those hoarded points are still waiting to be given at the end of the period, the giver will look for any excuse to recognize someone and use up the points. ("Oh, no! I still haven't used my points to recognize anyone! Julie brought me a cup of coffee when she came into the meeting. I'll recognize her for 'teamwork' for that.")

Touch as Many People as Possible, as Often as Possible

Social recognition creates a big winner's circle. In old-school recognition programs, a few people received large awards. Our partners have learned they can achieve substantial improvements by adding a lower range of awards with economic value to the program's portfolio. Often, this range includes five to six award levels, beginning with an award with an economic value of $25 to $50, then increasing at standard increments to a top economic value of $1,000. Giving many small awards in addition to a smaller number of larger-denomination awards allows vastly higher penetration rates for your recognition program than large awards alone.

Companies have a bell curve of performance. There will always be an elite 10 percent of high-performing employees. If you recognize only that top 10 percent, then essentially the same group of people will get celebrated year after year. They'll receive big bonuses, take the trips to Hawaii, and so on. They're also the only employees whose behavior is positively reinforced by recognition.

Here's why that approach means lost opportunity: That particular group of people already wakes up every morning very motivated to do their jobs. It's important to recognize high performers, but if you confine your recognition program to them, you create a very small winner's circle—one already inhabited by engaged, motivated employees.

Social recognition rewards that top 10 percent (and they will still get the lion's share of the high-value awards). It also recognizes the 70 percent of people behind those top performers who carry the organization every day. These are the classic unsung heroes. They are the "Mighty Middle"—the people who dutifully attend to their tasks, are consistently polite on the phone, and reliably complete work on time. A broad improvement in company performance requires bringing these people into the winner's circle.

It's simple logic: raising the engagement of a majority of employees will result in outsized performance improvements. To imagine otherwise is to waste that middle 70 percent's potential. Furthermore, even though individuals in that middle 70 percent might not create spectacular break-throughs, they are the foundation and support that make breakthroughs by the elites possible and profitable.

Finally, that middle 70 percent constitutes the social architecture of the company. They are most likely to recognize the elites, and the most likely to spread enthusiasm, engagement, and positivity among them-selves. They are the carriers of social recognition and, by extension, your culture. And they deserve to be recognized as well. The bottom-line prin-ciple for effective social recognition is that everyone is eligible to give and receive recognition for a job well done.

Frequent awards are the result of wide participation, and the two inspire each other in a virtuous cycle. According to our case study produced with the Stanford School of Business, when 5 to 8 percent of employees receive some form of recognition every week, the program reaches a tipping point: most employees know the program and embrace its goals.[7] In practice, some employees will receive two awards in a year, and some will receive six. The study further recommends a program goal of 80 percent reach, that is, eight out of 10 employees will receive at least some recognition during the year. (To those who doubt 80 percent of employees deserve some recognition during the year, we respond: Is your employee base truly that disengaged? In our experience, the problem is not disengagement but lack of recognition for the many small and large contributions of the typical employee.)

Frequent small awards also align with worldwide social media habits—the trend toward touch points that are both frequent and brief (think Twitter, Facebook, and Vine as well as texting).

MYTHBUSTER
Managers should be the focal point for giving recognition

Managers matter. Managers noticing and appreciating the work of the members of their team is necessary and important to employee engagement. We all need to know that our manager sees our good work, our successes, and our daily victories. But even the very best managers cannot see all the good that is happening around them every day. That's why empowering all employees to "catch someone doing something good" and recognize him or her for it is critical to recognition program success. Indeed, it doesn't become truly social until all employees are on the lookout for the praiseworthy and then, well, praising it.

Frequent awards don't break the budget when managed in a professionally designed system that scales recognition awards across a wide range of monetary value. For example, most customers use a mix of noncash awards redeemable for an economic value of $25/$50, $100, $500, and $1,000. This flexibility allows for frequent small awards and less frequent large awards. The average value of individual awards is approximately $100, with yearly total award spending of about $250 per employee.

Awards given to teams create a larger winner's circle, as more individuals participate while reinforcing the message that teamwork counts. When awarding a team, structure the award so that individuals receive equivalent awards and make the recognition moment a group event. (With a standard of living index controlling the monetary value of awards according to geography, cost of living, currency values, and so on, the awards can be equitable across a global enterprise.)

A recognition program with frequent awards also creates immediacy. Managers can create recognition moments quickly, tying the recognition and reward to behavior that's fresh in memory. We call this "high-speed recognition"because managers don't have to wait for the perfect moment or dither about whether the moment will be visible to all (the recognition moment can be repeated later, if needed).

Spontaneity adds impact and fun to a recognition program. Keeping the recognition moment simple ensures that everyone understands how it works. Combined with frequent communications, these many, little, surprising moments create buzz around the program. This approach brings company values alive for the rank-and-file as a nonstop narrative of recognition illustrates the connection between company values and employee behavior. Soon, the program creates a thousand little stories of engaged employees being honored—what they did and, critically, why it mattered. This is how positivity spreads through the work to create a Positivity Dominated Workplace.

Which employee actions your managers recognize depends on the culture, values, and priorities of your company. Here is a list of examples:

- Exhibiting behavior aligned to company values
- Going above job requirements
- High-performing teams (recognize everyone on the team!)
- Passing a milestone
- Surpassing quality targets in a product or process
- Accountability (accepting responsibility and keeping promises)
- Customer service brilliance (measured by time to resolution, customer ratings, etc.)
- Promoting company values to the community
- Innovation (in products or ways of doing things)
- Initiative (not waiting to get started on a great idea)
- Leadership
- Inclusion and encouraging diversity of opinion or background

- Employee referrals
- Mentoring new employees
- Volunteering time to company-supported charities or good works

> *Shorthand for managers: if you would have said,*
> *"Thank you!" that's a recognition moment.*

Remember the power that stories have to inspire managers and raise the profile of the recognition program. As your social recognition initiative launches, share examples of how company values are being recognized and rewarded. Circle back to your managers, asking them to expand a company-wide "knowledge base" of what actions they recognize and why they are simultaneously important to employees and the bottom line.

Calibrate Awards to Match Achievements

In an organization where merit matters, awards vary to match the size of the achievement being recognized. People crave affirmation that their actions are important and meaningful, but they understand that actions have different effects on the bottom line.

At the outset of a recognition program, managers are correctly concerned about deciding on the size of awards and ensuring equity among employees. While we've said that the praise matters more than the prize, nominators for recognition still need guidelines. These can be set early in the design of the program, bearing in mind factors like budget, the differing value of awards across geographic regions ($100 buys more in Mumbai or Memphis than it buys in Manhattan), and the need to include all deserving employees.

Employees should have a simple concept of how different awards levels are set. One model: Award level A = extra contribution with immediate impact; Award level B = unusually strong contribution or unusually tough challenge met with lasting impact; Award level C = extraordinary contribution with profound impact.

Here is a list of best practices for setting your award guidelines:

- Keep the number of award levels as simple as possible.
- Establish award levels that relate easily to the degree of the employee's contribution or achievement.
- Ensure that the award values are substantially different to simplify the nominator's choice.
- Provide corresponding examples of behavior for each award level for consistency of awards on a global basis.
- Keep in mind that the appropriate currency for a "compensation strategy" is cash, whereas the appropriate currency for a "recognition strategy" must be noncash.

To ensure equity and management of the recognition program without bogging down the program, do the following:

- Keep the number of approval levels to a minimum to ensure speedy award approval and to make sure the award is issued as close as possible to the time that the behavior was exhibited for maximum impact.
- If possible, set a range of awards that managers of different levels can make spontaneously without asking for permission. Set and monitor the total number of awards budgeted.
- All awards must be tracked and reported upon; therefore, approvals should not become a barrier to wide use of awards.
- Low-value and peer-to-peer awards should require no approvals, where possible.

Be alert to the pros and cons of approval processes. While it's logical for your organization to establish guidelines for approving the spending on awards, don't let an approval chain delay most awards, because speedily recognizing behavior is very powerful. If the COO has to approve most awards, that will take time and the award will lose some of its impact; furthermore, the message such delays send (that the manager who decides on an award needs to ask permission) can be counterproductive to the whole program.

Simple approval levels are almost always best for the great majority of awards in a high-penetration recognition program. Requiring nominators to get just one sign-off on their awards should be adequate in most cases, except for the highest-value awards.

Adoption

Any new initiative requires a critical mass of adoption by employees to achieve its goals, and that's doubly true of a social initiative like recognition. Quick adoption by a large number of employees means better ROI for the program over time, and faster results in terms of engagement, energy and performance.

Promote It or Perish

Engagement, excitement, and education are your goals, so use your organization's best communicators in a three-phase process around the launch of your program:

Phase 1: Prelaunch—Create Anticipation and Enthusiasm

- Create a "stealth" secure social media presence internally, with messages posted by staff, educating and reminding employees about the upcoming launch. If your company intranet is heavily used, do it there. Otherwise, use organization-private social media like Chatter, Jive, or Yammer.
- "Tease" the program with personalized communication from the CEO and program leader to all employees, explaining the meaning and importance of the program.
- Distribute network-based reminders about the launch of the program (such as screen savers and/or a running electronic "zipper" display in the lobby, each describing a value to recognize).
- Set expectations with personalized voice mails or texts from the CEO to division heads.

- Hold a web meeting with all division heads featuring top executives endorsing the program.
- Publish statements from managers testifying to their anticipation of the launch of the program; include managers who have used social networking in previous jobs.
- Be sure offline employees are equally involved through posters, flyers, digital signage, and start-of-shift meeting scripts for managers.

As part of your early messaging, describe to all employees how managers and even line staff will be held accountable for implementing social recognition. This goes beyond a supportive "let's all do our best" message. Have the CEO kick off the program at a public event, publicized well in advance. It's surprising the uplift you'll get from publicly stating that this program is important enough to the company that you're rolling it out like all other major initiatives. (When the CEO has gone public with a launch date, the team gets motivated to hit that date and everything goes much more smoothly.)

Phase 2: Launch—Educate and Inspire Early Adoption

- Send a mass text message or voice mail to all employees on the day of launch.
- Send an animated e-mail, linked to a video announcement including the principal program sponsor and the CEO.
- Release a video of executives describing how the recognition program affects everyone in the company and drives company culture.
- Include news stories on your intranet announcing the program and its goals and expectations for use and participation by all employees.
- Send out a public press release announcing the program.
- Announce contests such as an e-mail nomination campaign.
- Global companies: host a worldwide launch event.

On launch day, you'll get a quadruple benefit by giving a small award (of say, $25 or $50 in economic value) to everyone. First, everybody in the company immediately knows about the program—and knows it's serious because you just spent money in the best way. Second, everyone experiences the pleasure of receiving an award; experience is much more memorable than, say, an e-mail describing the program. Third, they get trained: They know what an award looks like. They have an award to redeem, so they have to go to the recognition website and go through the process of redeeming it. And the fourth benefit is that you build morale because you've just given everybody in the company a gift.

Phase 3: Postlaunch and Ongoing—Remind and Integrate with Daily Activities

- Launch an internal social media page or feed dedicated to celebrating recognition awards, including interviews with employees who have received awards!
- Launch a recognition news feed that is like Facebook or other popular social media in style and orientation, but secure within your organization.
- Hold informal chats about the program via social networks like Chatter and Yammer.
- At regular company meetings, have managers who have used social recognition to improve performance tell their stories. Include this with other success stories (sales, product launches, marketing campaigns).
- Run a contest for stories of how receiving and giving recognition affected the individual.
- Conduct periodic reporting and showcase results of the program at 3-, 6- and 12-month anniversaries, or keep a running tally of awards on the company intranet.

You need to brand your recognition program. When recognition program leaders tell us they struggle to get their message out and unify employees behind their corporate mission, we ask first, "What do you call your program?" Sometimes the name is nothing more than a label: "Acme Corporation Recognition Program." At the other extreme, we've seen companies with dozens of different names for dozens of different recognition programs, all with names made up by local managers, creating brand chaos.

We advocate a single, unique brand identity for a company's social recognition program. Creating a unified brand promotes unity across divisions and borders. With one name known by everyone, the company has a one-company voice and a one-company mission around which employees can rally. Branding your social recognition program in this kind of disciplined yet creative way is a chance to reinforce key values that make the company unique. As in consumer marketing, the brand ties multiple positive messages and emotional "hooks" into a single name, and strong branding helps make the program memorable for the long term.

> *A company's social recognition program should have a single, unique brand.*

Additional positive effects of a single brand include:

- *Efficiency in marketing.* In a global company, multiple brands for the recognition program require duplicating design, collateral materials, messaging, and so on. We have encountered companies with as many as 20 separate recognition efforts with multiple names, which is confusing as well as wasteful.
- *Unity.* One brand across multiple business divisions promotes united effort and breaks down walls of geography and status. Everyone in every division who acts according to company values deserves recognition.
- *Culture reinforcement.* One brand, carefully chosen to speak about company values, reinforces the company's culture.

Our global customers that work in multiple languages wonder if a single brand can be effective around the world. Creating that strong, single brand is a powerful way to unite all employees behind one phrase, one belief, and one approach. The company can use a common-language term—such as "Eureka!" or "Bravo!"—that is widely known (even in Asia and the Middle East). Some of our customers have enjoyed the reinforcing power of choosing a name related to the business (an energy company choosing "Energize!" or JetBlue's charming play on words, "Lift"). Less commonly, a company with worldwide operations might make up a name for its recognition program tied to the company name along the lines of "ACME+You."

Recognition-program managers should plan to meet early on with the brand managers and the marketing department of their company and together find a strong name for the program that conveys a message to wrap around the promise of your program.

Social recognition shares the cadence of social networking, and as we've seen in networks like Facebook and LinkedIn, regular participation unleashes its full potential. You will have to "socialize" the new program across the enterprise. This is no small matter—it really amounts to change management, whether you are instituting a new program, replacing an old one, or upgrading to a more useful system.

You're introducing a new habit to busy people, and that poses a challenge: even when employees know the importance of social recognition, and even when they enjoy it, the habit is unfamiliar. Your promotion of the practice will prime the pump for that activity, and that means the early days of the program require frequent repetition of your core messages.

Fortunately, the social nature of recognition means that its use is inherently self-promoting. When I give an award, my manager has to approve it, and so is alerted to the behavior that inspires that award. After the award is given, it's clearly visible to the immediate team around the recipient, and social channels within the company (especially online channels such as the company awards feed) propagate the message. If 5 percent of the workforce receives an award over the course of a week, a huge percentage of the workforce hears about it, learns a bit more about the program, and perhaps looks a little harder for behavior to recognize. Awareness becomes self-perpetuating in a short time.

But that only happens if your initial promotion primes the pump. That means following up a strong launch with messages over the course of at least a year. Over time, the message will change from educating employees about the program and its goals to inspiring participation with success stories. This change, incidentally, helps build the Positivity Dominated Workplace we described in Chapter 2.

Launching social recognition calls for a *high frequency*, *high impact*, and *multifaceted* communications program. You want to raise program awareness continuously, and the need for that is familiar to anyone who has worked to change the habitual practices of a workforce.

Employees should receive seven to eight messages about the program in a short period around the launch. We've learned that 85 percent of successful recognition programs touch employees every two weeks in a variety of ways, including testimonials, success stories, training brush-ups, employee endorsements, and bright visual communication like posters and short video messages.

Eight Fatal Signs of a Poor Recognition Program

The Ascent Group, a management consultancy, ranks these qualities as characteristic of the worst recognition programs. Plan them out of your program![8]

- Inconsistency
- Untimely recognition or reward delivery
- Unclear program qualifications or criteria
- Perceived unattainable goals or uncontrollable goals
- Rewards don't match employee desires; limited choice or undervalued rewards
- Programs that don't include all employee classifications
- Programs with few winners
- Catalog award selection is limited

Train Managers and Celebrate Recognition Moments

When implementing a recognition program, employees will require training in how the program works. Telling employees about the mechanics of the program—what it is, where to log in to nominate or redeem an award, how to use an online advisor to recommend appropriate award levels, and so forth—is the easy part. (In a global company, this might also include information about tax considerations or budgets and changes to accommodate language, local business customs, and cultural cues—all fairly easy to adapt.)

But showing managers how and when to create recognition moments—and why doing it well is important to team, division, and company success—requires another layer of training. We've seen that this is actually even simpler than the mechanics but causes much more anxiety over doing it right. People believe that because recognition is powerful, it's as difficult as other management disciplines.

This is a bit of a red herring. People understand the fundamental act of recognizing achievement, and the breathtaking pace of social media adoption worldwide affirms a natural human need for social interaction of all kinds.

Your managers haven't earned an MBA in recognition, but they're not children, either. It's not their job to entertain employees, and not everyone needs a high level of emotional intelligence for recognition to work. Employees already know their managers' temperaments. As long as a manager's appreciation is sincere, fair, and deserved, employees will get the message. While training can help the less socially adept manager's use of recognition, training should also focus on managing social recognition as a management discipline systematically across divisions, locations, and cultures.

Summarize training by telling managers, "Catch your people doing the right thing." That said, there are several good ways to reinforce the essentials of social recognition:

- Teach mechanics, such as the hands-on operation of the recognition approval and reporting system, an easy mobile app for real-time approvals and nominations, using every method available, including efficiencies like web-based interactive training.

- Train the trainers to understand the business implications of recognition and the stages of the recognition journey, from tactical recognition all the way to talent management (see Chapter 5).
- Make training social as well: Encourage all to participate, comment, and, especially, to add stories and scenarios in which recognition can advance company goals.
- When choosing between speed and formality of recognition, choose speed. Launch the program and watch your managers figure it out as they try to hit their awards targets.
- Include baseline recognition practices for all training of new managers and in your ongoing leadership development courses.
- Teach specific recognition techniques. For example, every recognition award should include very specific praise that makes explicit the connection among behaviors, values, and company goals.
- Teach recognition habits. For example, every recognition award should be followed up with reinforcing praise and congratulations, in person whenever possible.
- Have managers who are especially talented at recognition act as mentors to others and ambassadors of the recognition program as a way to maintain everyone's enthusiasm and improve their recognition skills.
- Collect and communicate real-world accounts of recognition moments throughout the company—train by example!

Continue the enthusiasm generated in training through your ongoing communications program. Remember, while training can instill new skills, managers will make recognition a daily practice only if they are convinced it brings results, so broadcast those results in e-mails, newsletters, and ongoing management training.

Monitor your progress with follow up training where necessary. If your program is tracking recognition activity, the program owner will quickly see where recognition is happening and where it's not. If you launch a program and let managers know they have to hit a target number of awards given, as we've suggested, their awareness of value-affirming behaviors grows.

Be sure, too, to include training in onboarding for all new employees. This serves as an excellent introduction to your company's culture of recognition as well as to the program itself. The power of thanks and recognition program mechanisms should also be included in any ongoing manager leadership and development training programs.

Say "recognition moment," and our customers first imagine a ceremony where the entire department stands around and the manager gives out awards. Picturing this, and then thinking about achieving a high penetration rate in which 5 percent of the workforce is recognized every two weeks, our customers rightfully worry that there will be so many ceremonies that nobody gets any work done!

Actually, the recognition moment is when an employee receives an award and, more important, *receives the personal message that accompanies the award.* That moment can happen publicly or privately, in person, via e-mail, in a ceremony, or even at home via ordinary delivered mail. There are many options.

Three points matter: The award is linked to a values- and goals-based activity, it's made quickly after the activity occurs, and somebody has taken time to write a personal message describing why the activity matters. The personal effort to write a message gives the award emotional impact.

Ceremonies delay the recognition moment and separate it from the activity that earned it, which reduces the impact of the award, in addition to taking more time and sometimes becoming less personal.

There is a place for ceremonies in a recognition program. Ceremonies are good for large team accomplishments, when many people are being rewarded. Little ceremonies might be scheduled into the work routine, for example when a manager reads the names and achievements of reward recipients at the end of a weekly team meeting. In a large company, an e-mail or webcast might be broadcast periodically celebrating employee accomplishments large and small. (Again, this helps promote the recognition program and remind employees of company values.) Push communications integrated into the program to promote recognition received by a team on a weekly basis accomplishes the same goal.

A social recognition platform is an ongoing celebration of accomplishments, values, and positivity, which is yet another reason to make your recognition program as social as possible.

Be aware that public ceremonies aren't everyone's cup of tea. A recognition ceremony for an introverted person can be agonizing, which is more punishment than reward. Managers need to exercise judgment when choosing public versus private recognition.

MYTHBUSTER
Public recognition is always best

A public recognition ceremony can in some cases be counter-productive. Focus on the substance of the recognition—the personal message, the achievements being recognized, and the timing of the award—rather than the style of presentation. The cadence of public versus private recognition can vary depending on temperaments, working conditions, and company traditions.

A guiding slogan for effective recognition moments is *It's about the praise and not the prize.* It's about the manager conferring psychic income clearly, directly, and quickly. It's about strengthening relationships among team members and between managers and staff. Yes, the material award is important, but the recognition moment itself is primarily about psychic income—prestige, self-confidence, group cohesion, and pride.

Social recognition leverages your company's social architecture to help every employee perform at his or her best. Managers find themselves having a new conversation with employees about how their individual actions build financial and cultural value. Peers reinforce the message in conversation, e-mail, and behavior, all at a pace and in styles that have evolved over time through social work relationships.

The recognition moment is also a great moment of communication—positive feedback that can lead to a richer dialogue between manager and staff. Even if the moment has to come by e-mail, the employee's response to the manager is a connection.

> *Social recognition is more about the praise than the prize.*

Recognition is a wonderful tool for making sure there is positive conversation between managers and employees. The implicit message: "I am recognizing *you* because you did something recently that contributed to the company in the following way. I want to make certain you know that I and others notice, approve, and appreciate what you did."

A Guide to Recognition Moments

Not every manager is blessed with the warmth or personal presence to deliver the recognition message perfectly, but that hardly matters. We have found there are several important behaviors to bring to the moment:

- Make the presentation culturally appropriate, especially in international divisions of global companies.
- Always tie the act being recognized to a specific company value and to a long-term strategy.
- Convey the reason for recognition as a story. One classic format is known as SAR (you faced this *Situation*, took this *Action*, and got this *Result*).
- Tell how you feel about the employee, such as appreciative, approving, proud, gratified, and glad to have him or her on your team.
- Check details before the moment occurs, such as name spellings and pronunciations, dates, manager and team members, and the division's big goals and/or targets.

> ■ Celebrate winners and winning but do not create a "class system" of winners and losers. Everyone aware of the recognition must believe he or she is eligible for the same reward.
>
> Focus on the inherent value of the employee's actions, not on the material value of the award.

Rewards

The era of the gold watch is long gone, so consider a few principles when determining the nature and size of rewards in a social recognition program.

Offer a Great Choice of Rewards

Employees are individuals—this is a fundamental principle of social recognition. Each employee makes unique contributions, has unique tastes, and desires uniqueness. The best managers, and indeed the best global organizations, learn that rewards are most effective when they honor the individual.

Here is where vendors of old-fashioned recognition programs operate using a flawed business model. Their revenues derive chiefly from selling only preselected merchandise, which cannot cater to so many unique individuals. This business model dilutes social recognition's core belief that it's about the praise and not the prize, because old-fashioned recognition is prominently tied to the prize.

Today's global organization has a multigenerational, multigeographic employee base—a vast range of tastes and values in which everyone from Shanghai to Savannah to Stockholm feels he or she should have a rich choice of rewards. Even the largest merchandise-based programs are limited in their offerings to the range of products being selected by a purchasing agent working for an incentive company, and managers or leaders make a classic mistake when they think that they can choose rewards that will be appreciated by everyone.

Merchandise-only programs were designed before the advent of the multicultural, global organization, and they make little allowance for differences among cultures. A crystal trophy might sit well on a desk in Paris, but does it have the same meaning in Toronto or Miami?

MYTHBUSTER
Cash Is Not King

The following table contrasts cash versus noncash rewards (such as gift cards and points). We find that cash is easily forgotten or spent on necessities, which makes the award unmemorable and thus ineffective.

CASH REWARDS	NONCASH REWARDS
Cannot be discussed with others Becomes an entitlement Is easily spent on necessities ■ Bills – 29% ■ Do not remember – 18% ■ Never received a cash reward – 15%	Fulfills wants and creates memories Reinforces commitment to the company Provides "trophy value" tangible symbol Are socially acceptable to brag about Provides guilt-free reward enjoyment Delivers a higher perceived value

The Internet has created a world of choice for all consumers, including your employees. With literally millions of objects available at the click of a mouse, consumers have become extraordinarily brand- and cost-conscious, and they expect a wide range of choice in everything from music to clothes to restaurants to travel. They also understand the value of a brand like Macy's department store, where a professional buyer can find items that are current, fashionable, and focused on the Macy's customer. Note that this includes experiences as well as items, and experiences create strong positive emotions for people. For many, a visit to a restaurant or spa can carry greater value than a new possession.

Social recognition embraces this trend and magnifies the moment of recognition with the power of choice. In a partnership of goodwill, the giver determines the value of the award, and the recipient determines the final object or experience awarded (typically through the use of merchant-specific gift cards globally as well as on-demand merchandise options). In this way, the recipient becomes a participant in his or her own recognition, not a passive-if-gratified spectator.

Imagine the conscious and unconscious thoughts of an employee who's just received such an award:

- Employee A shipped a critical product early last quarter, and her manager recognized the accomplishment with a nice award. How will she use it? Since she worked many nights and weekends to ship the product early and was absent from home a lot, perhaps she'll choose a spa visit or weekend getaway for herself and her spouse.
- Employee B travels constantly as part of his job, and he might want those new noise-cancelling headphones he has seen in airports. (He'll really enjoy them whenever he's trying to work on a flight while a fussy baby shrieks three seats away.)
- Employee C receives an award and enjoys speculating on what to choose: Maybe he wants to get high-end football cleats for his child with a gift card to Zappos.com or GigaSports. Perhaps his daughter will need a dressy blazer for her new job—he can get that with a gift card to women's clothing retailer Ann Taylor. Every time he contemplates one of these choices, he subtly relives the meaning of the award—the recognition, appreciation, and connection to value-based performance.

In these examples, the critical factor is that the recipient has the gift of choice. Most items can be chosen either as gift cards to local merchants so the recipient can touch, feel, and choose directly, or as merchandise rewards for quick selection and redemption.

A Pocket Summary of Best Practices

1. Create one universal program.
2. Level the recognition field.
3. Publicize a broad winner's circle, from top performers to inspired "average" employees.
4. Give timely, specific recognition.
5. Link recognition moments to company core values and objectives.
6. Gain support of senior-level executive champions.
7. Invest 1 to 2 percent or more of payroll.
8. Go mobile! Put recognition technology in the palms of their hands.
9. Leverage your crowdsourced data.
10. Provide proportionate, local awards for all regions.
11. Brand your culture.
12. Include video recognition for how information is consumed today.
13. Leave cash off the table; offer a broad choice of awards.
14. Communicate and train your people.
15. Make it social. Make it peer-to-peer.
16. Monitor and measure.

Are You Ready?

In the Introduction, we asked, "Where are you on the recognition journey?" Whether you are a complete stranger contemplating social recognition for the first time or an experienced traveler looking to advance a strategic practice, the best first step is assessment. The best assessment of your organization is to identify the "speed bumps" in the journey, those risks that can slow down implementation and value creation anywhere along the journey.

This exercise is an assessment (not a test) of where potential problems for implementing social recognition exist in your organization. Rate each statement below as it applies to your organization. Use the following ratings:

5—Strongly Agree
4—Somewhat Agree
3—Neutral
2—Somewhat Disagree
1—Strongly Disagree

1. ___Managers have a good understanding of how to effectively recognize employees.
2. ___The organization has a history of successfully launching new initiatives.
3. ___Employees have a relatively high understanding of recognition and what behaviors should be rewarded.
4. ___There is a commitment to invest in a new recognition program.
5. ___Implementing a new program would be seen as a positive, not a threat.
6. ___This program would be fully supported by senior leadership.
7. ___There are no hard barriers to offering a recognition program.
8. ___There is an agreed sense of need for a recognition program.

Any statement about the organization you have rated 1 to 3 indicates an area that needs special attention during the planning and implementation process. It is wise to create detail around these speed bumps. For example, if you strongly disagree that there is a commitment to invest in a new recognition program, you will have to win executive commitment by developing a business case for recognition directly related to strategic goals. Is the problem that executives require financial proof of recognition's value? Present the data and models we've cited from researchers and customers, and create the business case elements we describe in Chapter 8.

When you've identified the risks, devote planning and implementation resources accordingly. The hidden value of this exercise is to help you think twice about the risks. For example, you might assume that managers have a good understanding of how to effectively recognize employees, especially if you've had a tactical recognition program in the past, but test that assumption around the company. Do employees generally feel their managers recognize their contributions? Are individual managers superstars at recognition? Enlist them as advocates and trainers for those who are behind the curve.

The "Green Light" List

We've seen strategically designed social recognition work around the world because it includes both the realities of today's corporations and the mindset of today's employees. Almost any recognition program brings benefits, but a program that is planned, launched, and operated as a major management initiative brings competitive advantage in abundance. In a world where most HR tools have been commoditized, why would a business striving to compete do anything less?

As you prepare to design and launch a program of social recognition, review the following checklist of essential building blocks of a truly successful recognition program. Double-check that these five elements of your program are in place. When they are, you can give the green light to the program launch.

1. The Stated Vision Tracked Through Executive and Manager Dashboards

Confirm that you have stated the overall, global vision for the program and described, in metric or KPI form, your program's targets. These can be something like "Improve employee engagement scores from current levels by 10 percent," "Increase employee satisfaction scores around recognition and appreciation by 20 percent," "Achieve employee satisfaction scores related to recognition of 85 percent," "Reduce voluntary turnover by 12 percent," "Achieve Q12 scores of X," and so on. Then create an executive dashboard report that uses real data to monitor progress in meeting the targets established. The report should list the company-wide "vision" metrics at the top and the nuts-and-bolts metrics in graph form underneath (these include overall penetration levels, penetration of each division or department, values adoption as represented by recognition, talent management implications, and operational necessities such as award approval/disapproval levels, enterprise budget targets, etc.). To take this one step further, draft an executive dashboard report with the data you anticipate six months after the recognition program has been launched. When you get to that date, compare the projection with the reality.

2. Core Values Distribution Analysis

Generate values distribution analysis charts from the data you collect. Executive leaders agree to monitor it and take corrective action if the results identify any problems. As we've said, social recognition's value can lie in revealing which core values are lacking as well as which are abundant. It is essential that there is a strong correlation between all awards and company values. If there are some global, all-company, business initiatives (e.g., Six Sigma), then these can be added to the core values as award reasons.

3. Executive Sponsor

Make sure there are one or more executive sponsors in place to ensure the social recognition program delivers what it promises. The executive sponsors will need to agree to monitor and discuss the quarterly executive dashboard and take any corrective action needed. Of course, they cannot do this if they have not been empowered by top leadership to do so, and they will not be effective if they do not agree with the targets that have been established. Often the head of HR is one of the executive sponsors, but there should also be someone from another division of the company.

4. *Leader Accountability*

At an operational level, program metrics must be broken down into relevant targets for each division, department, country leader, or grouping (depending on the company). These leaders could be the people who approve the awards, for example. Without targets, these leaders will not have true accountability for the success of the recognition program. These leaders will have their individual activity metrics communicated to them and will be accountable for monitoring progress. Ideally, this accountability for the recognition program will be included in the management by objectives plans for these managers. By setting targets for recognition in their departments, reviewing recognition metrics regularly, and tweaking the program as necessary, companies can make the social recognition program become a natural part of the management rhythm.

5. *True Social Design*

To harvest the benefits of social recognition, you'll need a recognition program design that powerfully encourages the mass mobilization of your employees' eyes to notice the good work happening around them every day and raise their voices to express thanks. Have you included multiple, differentiated award levels that are open to all to nominate? Is peer-to-peer recognition encouraged sufficiently? Do you have natural social enablers that ensure your initiative becomes self-sustaining, like a news feed, activity digests, and opportunities for all to congratulate others on the recognition they've received?

This chapter can serve as an "Instruction Manual" for building a social recognition program. It's a long chapter because, like any strategic initiative, social recognition requires careful thought, planning and execution. Earlier, we discussed the good business reasons for having a program in the first place, and in the next chapter, we'll explore several additional ways in which social recognition drives ROI and business results.

8 | Driving ROI and Business Results

Mark Berry likes thinking about data. The Vice President of People Insights at ConAgra Foods runs one of the most far-reaching and exciting HR data practices we've seen, and part of his job is using recognition data to predict business needs.

"We have aggregated five years of employee information, adding about two million rows of data to that database daily," says Berry. "We're able to look at demographics like compensation, performance, and ratings of employee potential, and then tie those to recognition."

Berry's practice expands the business value of recognition well beyond HR issues. He says, "I have three industrial-organizational psychologists on my team who do strictly predictive or inferential data analytics. They study the data with questions like: What are people being recognized for? Who is initiating recognition—is it a team leader, a peer, or someone from another team? What's the frequency of recognition? Then we tie that information to other analytics to find predictive properties in the data. . . . At the end of last year we released an attrition prediction algorithm. It clearly shows us that the failure to recognize good performers is a guarantee those good performers will leave."

Recognition data analysis yields insights that confirm anecdotal truths about the practice. "We find that, especially as career level increases, monetary recognition alone doesn't mitigate the absence of other recognition," Berry observes. "People like having the money, but they want to know they're appreciated for what they do and they're valued as part of the organization. Money without [appreciation] will not mitigate attrition risk."

* * *

What really drives financial success? Two social scientists from Gallup and The University of Iowa set out to find the answer by conducting a meta-analysis using data from 2,178 business units in 10 large organizations. Their study found that "engaged employees cause high retention rates, better financial performance, and customer loyalty."

Adding detail to such findings, Gallup's 2013 Global Workplace report confirms the stark differences between companies with more or less engaged workers. The median difference between a company with a very engaged workforce and one with an unengaged workforce covers the range of success measures, for example:

- 21 percent higher productivity
- 22 percent higher profitability
- 41 percent higher quality (fewer defects)
- 48 percent fewer safety incidents
- 37 percent reduced absenteeism
- 10 percent higher customer ratings[1]

In Chapter 3 we showed how recognition leads to engagement, energy, and enthusiasm across a workforce. Executives have a gut feel for the positive outcomes that result. In this chapter, we'll take a look at additional business reasons to make recognition a strategic imperative. As we've seen, a recognition practice is an enabling technology for engagement, building trust, connection, cohesion, and happiness at work. Those are the kind of qualities that lead to the results Gallup's researchers find year after year.

Business leaders choose among many practices and initiatives, and the key question before dedicating budget to a practice is whether it will produce a satisfactory return on investment. Recognition's results appear in a direct line from the individual recognition moment (a more satisfied, engaged employee) and from the social network effects of many such moments. The outcomes that indicate a payoff are found in directly related metrics like improved retention rates, indirectly related benefits like those named a best place to work, and benefits enabled by the technology of a recognition practice.

Newer research also finds secondary—but clearly related and tangible—benefits related to recognition programs, such as an improved stock price.[2]

If a recognition practice sets funding at 1 percent of payroll, then the return of these primary and secondary benefits can and should be measured against that cost. Let's examine them.

Research Insight

Two social scientists examining Gallup's ongoing metadata studies asked the chicken-or-egg question of whether engagement leads to profits or vice versa. They wrote, "We find that the path from the individual engagement elements to financial performance is stronger than the path from financial performance to engagement."[3]

Put engagement first and the profits will follow.

Reducing Turnover

Turnover is a budget-killer for HR because the cost of replacing employees who quit ranges from 50 percent to 150 percent of a year's salary.[4] For example, a company of 10,000 employees with annual salaries ranging between $30,000 and $150,000 and an 11 percent turnover rate spends more than $41 million in turnover costs! (See Figure 8.1.)

CALCULATING TURNOVER COSTS

We profiled a sample company of 10,000 employees with a very conservative 11% annual turnover rate and an average cost to replace of 75%

Company with 10,000 Employees

70%

10%

20%

Entry Level | Mid-mgmt | Senior mgmt

Average Annual Salaries

$30K $70K $150K

Cost to Replace (@75% of salary)

$22.5K $52.5K $112.5K

Annual Loss of Talent (@11% turnover)

770 people   220 people   110 people

$17.3 MM $11.6 MM $12.4 MM

$41.3MM

in bottom-line turnover costs

Figure 8.1 Calculating turnover costs

Compare that to the cost of a recognition program set at 1 percent of payroll ($4 million). Even if a recognition program reduced turnover by just 20 percent, it would more than pay for itself—and that doesn't include all the other benefits of recognition.[5]

Do the math with your company's payroll in mind; you'll know what turnover is costing you and what you can do about it. Social recognition pays for itself.

Becoming a Best Place to Work

China Gorman is the CEO of the Great Place to Work® Institute, the research and consulting firm that publishes the annual "100 Best Companies to Work For" list (with *Fortune* magazine). Her capsule description of a great workplace is one in which employees trust management, enjoy camaraderie with fellow workers, and feel pride in their work. Those fundamental qualities haven't changed since the Institute began its surveys in the early 1980s. Through all the changes in global business conditions, across the diverse priorities of generations, employees tell the Institute that those three factors are decisive in their assessment of a workplace. Trust, camaraderie, and pride thrive in companies as different in style as funky, funny Zappos and buttoned-down Boeing.

And they are all directly encouraged by social recognition. *Trust* is earned when management shows credibility, fairness, and respect for employees, and it grows (especially in the area of respect) when sincere appreciation is given and received. *Camaraderie*, the factor that means enjoying interaction with fellow employees, grows in the giving and receiving of praise and thanks among employees regardless of status. *Pride* is nurtured by the affirmation that what you do matters—the basis of recognition for a job well done.

What is the financial benefit of being a great place to work? Gorman offers some statistics contrasting the performance of the 100 Best Companies against the U.S. average:[6]

Turnover among the 100 best companies ranges from 50 percent to 65 percent lower than the U.S. median. Gorman says, "If you go no further investing in your culture [than] to retain your employees, it pays off in dollars and cents on the bottom line because your turnover will plummet." Reducing turnover through social recognition results in hard-dollar savings.

Headcount growth—an HR proxy for expanding business—of Best Companies is five times the rate of the US average (15.4 percent versus 3.2 percent). (These are big companies, not small start-ups who can double by adding 20 employees. Moreover they hire judiciously because salary and benefit costs are such a big part of the budget.)

A boost in reputation and recruiting comes with being on the list. Grace Soriano-Abad, vice president of global staffing at NetApp (a perennial presence on the 100 Best list) notes that every year when NetApp appears on the list, they see a 30 percent spike in resume submissions.[7] There's public relations value in local markets of being known as a great place to work, and the resulting employee pride is a self-reinforcing contribution to culture. Says Gorman, "Whether there truly is a talent shortage or not, CEOs understand that it's getting harder and harder to find the skills and the talent they need." Today, any advantage in recruiting has a direct benefit, and third-party validation helps a company's effort to attract talent.

Why Recognition Is like an Ultramarathon

When he's not running ConAgra Foods' employee data practice, Mark Berry runs ultramarathons. What's the similarity? He tells this story:

"I ran a 50 mile ultramarathon in the Flint Hills of Kansas. It was a very hilly course: a horrible, rocky, nasty surface. Dusty, hot, humid conditions with hailstorms threatening. What keeps you going at a time when you're teetering between getting to the finish line and going to the emergency room? It's that person who is standing there as you come into an aid station with 8 miles left. That person doesn't even know you, but they say, 'You're doing a great job. You look great. Just keep going. You're almost there.'

"In business we get busy, we get preoccupied, and we lose sight of what really wires people to work. Peer-to-peer [social recognition] affirms something. When someone says, 'Thanks! What you did means so much to me today,' it makes you want to hang in there."

Owning a Coveted Employer Brand

Fifteen years ago just a few visionaries in human resources used the term "employer brand." Now it's commonly understood as a critical part of recruiting. In a world where every candidate can receive 10 targeted job opportunities in a daily e-mail, employers rely more and more on a carefully crafted brand message to distinguish them from their competitors for talent. The distinctive employer brand attracts the right candidates to apply for jobs and decreases the cost of attracting candidates through advertising and other marketing efforts.

You already know the power of an employer brand when you say, "Everybody in tech wants to work at Google," or "For someone in consumer goods, Procter & Gamble is the place to be." You know it when you say, "Everyone on Wall Street aspires to be at Goldman Sachs," or "If sports are your life, you can't beat working at Nike." A brand is not just about salary, or size, or success, or even culture—it's about all of these and more. Branding pays off in recruiting because it creates momentum behind the message: More good people are attracted to the company, allowing the company to hire the best, which in turn drives success, which in turn drives reputation, which in turn attracts more good people. (Google gets roughly 250 applicants for every person it hires, and it only interviews the supremely qualified.)[8]

> *A brand is not just about salary, or size, or success,*
> *or even culture—it's about all these and more.*

Employer brands—like all brands—are built on three promises: tangible attributes (like pay and location), intangible attributes (like prestige and company culture), and reasons to believe (like being on a "best companies to work for" list). Social recognition contributes to all three in the following ways:

Tangible attributes of a recognition program include the economic value of social recognition awards. Although the awards vary in size and frequency, the tangible gift that comes with an award—whether it is a gift card at a desirable online boutique or a carefully chosen item—is not the "same" as salary, but it's quantifiable and very real at the moment of the award and later.

Intangible attributes conferred by a recognition program include all the qualities that social recognition contributes to workplace culture, such as shared values, pride, cohesion, and positivity. Bearing in mind that people leave jobs because of a lack of recognition, think about the intangible benefit to a company brand if a candidate knows, "At that company, my work will be appreciated." (Contrast that with the company where a potential candidate thinks, "My work won't be appreciated there," and you can imagine the power of intangible benefits.)

Reasons to believe are embedded in social recognition itself, which cultivates feelings of goodwill and camaraderie among employees, feelings that they make public in how they talk about the company. Increasingly, those feelings are shared online, in social media and on company reputation sites like Glassdoor. When it comes to authenticating your company's promise, one employee's enthusiastic thumbs-up, or one third-party award for being a superior place to work, is worth a thousand words of marketing copy.

You can quantify the benefit of becoming a coveted employer brand over time through improvements in standard recruiting data such as time to hire, number of qualified applicants, and quality of hire. Combined with the savings of improved turnover rate, these data points demonstrate the business case for social recognition. Becoming a talent magnet also blunts the threat of engaging in a "salary arms race" during tight labor markets or when competing with less well-regarded companies for exceptional talent. The best candidates don't just take a job for money; they want to do great work in a place that appreciates them.

The case for building a coveted employer brand is bigger than hard-dollar savings, because for many companies a strong employer brand also confers a "halo effect" internally and externally. Employees are proud to work at a place where everybody wants to work. And as recruiters at Whole Foods Market, Edward Jones, and Intuit will tell you, people like to buy products from companies with great employer brands as well. That goodwill probably can't be quantified for your calculations, but in the best sense of the word, it's incalculable.

Increasing Productivity

Companies are always trying to increase productivity, whether measured by the broadest financial assessments (revenue per employee) or narrower goals (number of patents granted per $1 million investment in R&D). Implicit in the increased engagement and energy brought about through recognition, productivity is one of the chief benefits our customers have experienced over time. In addition to the Gallup finding of 21 percent higher productivity in highly engaged workforces mentioned earlier, the Globoforce Summer 2013 Workforce Mood Tracker survey revealed details on this: 59 percent of employees recognized in a values-based program within the past month report a positive change in their productivity.

The data support this. At IHG, a 5 percent rise in employee engagement translates to 70 cents more revenue per available room per night—in a 200-room hotel that's a yearly revenue increase of $50,000.[9]

Revenue and Valuation

Tom McMullen is the leader North American Reward Practice for the Hay Group, a global management consulting firm. An expert on engagement, McMullen points out, "Recognition is one of the core drivers of engagement—along with career development opportunities and other rewards, a clear and promising direction, confidence in leaders [and] focus on customer." Hay Group's research shows that companies with top engagement scores show 2.5 times the revenue growth of companies with low scores.[10]

For public companies, revenue growth means a higher valuation in the market. The Parnassus Workplace Fund was founded by Jerome Dodson with the intention of investing only in large American companies that have also achieved distinction as employers, according to the employees themselves. The fund's managers started with a regression analysis comparing the "100 Best Places to Work" against the Standard & Poor's 500 index, and the analysis confirmed what they suspected: great workplaces beat the broader market. The fund bought into companies on the list, as well as others with outstanding workplace cultures. From the fund's inception in April 2005 to January 2013, the fund delivered an annualized return of 9.63 percent, compared to the S&P's 5.58 percent annualized return during that period.[11]

In an exhaustive analysis of the stock performance of companies on *Fortune*'s "100 Best Companies to Work For" list, Professor Alex Edmans of the Wharton School determined that they outperformed peers by 2 to 3 percent per year. In the paper's introduction, Edmans observed that "employee satisfaction is positively correlated with shareholder returns." He also recorded that the companies "also exhibited significantly more positive earnings surprises and stronger earnings announcement returns."[12]

> *Data show that employee satisfaction is positively correlated with shareholder returns.*

Data Analysis Magnifies Recognition's Contribution

Even if you aren't a data analytics ninja like Mark Berry, the information revealed by a social recognition program can extend recognition's value. Today, sophisticated data analytics are bringing employee management into a new age, and the data supplied by social recognition create a rich, real-time narrative of company life. By capturing and analyzing many individual acts of recognition, a social recognition practice can answer difficult questions like these:

- Who are the hidden influencers? Who has informal power, within the team and across the organization? Recognition data can pinpoint that go-to person in a technical field, or a gifted young graphic designer, whose influence is larger than his or her current position might indicate.
- Who has high potential? Employees with a lot of recognition from managers, peers, and staff (including people in different departments) have, in effect, a crowdsourced performance record.
- How are people connected via social networks in the workplace, as revealed by their observing and recognizing the work of others? For example, a customer sales representative who shows strong awareness of the technical implementation team through recognition shows an appreciation of the bigger picture, unlike someone with a "throw the problem over the fence" mindset.
- Where do the data conflict—for example, a person who is frequently recognized by peers but rarely by his manager?

Does that manager give many awards? Perhaps she doesn't participate in social recognition (and needs training or encouragement) or gives a lot of awards, but hasn't recognized the person who is frequently singled out by peers. That high-performing person could be a flight risk. Either way, the data reveal a red-flag situation long before it becomes a crisis.

- Who were the key performers in a particular project or initiative, as recognized by peers, managers, and staff? Frequent recognition creates a crowdsourced supplement to performance reviews, giving depth and real-time insight to behaviors that lead to success.
- What are the cultural differences among global locations as revealed in the number and types of awards and the values they promote?
- Where is recognition truly social (used freely and frequently by all, on fixed and mobile platforms, at any time), and where is it still stuck in an old top-down model (used only by managers, and only in the most rigid style)?

Because social recognition uncovers which values-based behaviors are lacking and which are abundant, you might think of it as a "brain scan" of company culture. With extensive data analysis, various constituencies can monitor their particular concerns:

Executives: What is my company culture? Is talent recognized appropriately? Are the values we promote top of mind for employees, and can they apply them to day-to-day work? Are we seeing increases in employee engagement, and how is this impacting our results in terms of sales growth or operating margin?

Managers: Is my team being recognized inside and outside the department? Who are my top performers, as chosen by those who work with them? What growth or development opportunities can I identify for my top performers based on the work at which they excel as shown by the recognition they receive?

Employees: Is my work valued, and by whom? Who else is being recognized, and for what? Which company values apply to my particular work? How does my work fit into the bigger picture of our organizational goals?

Human resources: Are we driving engagement, and where? What do employees value in each other? Who are the hidden high-potential employees and quiet influencers? Which areas in the organization are a potential concern?

Communication and Metrics Advice

Research and advisory firm Gartner adds some additional best practices to make a recognition program successful:[13]

- Capture baseline metrics across critical employee, customer and business performance measures, and continually monitor for impact and improvement.
- Invest in solutions that enable mobile access to the recognition platform, as these tools have a proven effect on increasing program participation and helping drive improved business outcomes.
- Look for social recognition tools that combine the benefits of intrinsic and extrinsic motivators. Extrinsic motivators (such as gift cards, points and other rewards) can be important reinforcements of intrinsic motivators (such as achievement, purpose and mastery).

In a strategically driven social recognition program, a strong correlation between recognition and the company values (plus key all-company strategic initiatives) is essential. They can be separated into two bar charts monitoring the traction of award activity (linked to behavior) for these initiatives.

Here's an example of one data set that reveals otherwise obscure information: the strength or weakness of certain values among divisions of a fictional company. The most important values of the company are respect, integrity, innovation, and teamwork. Figure 8.2 shows how often those values are recognized over three months.

Division 1 gives and receives few awards, most frequently for the value of respect. However, this happens to be the product development group. Why is there so little recognition of innovation? Do the managers believe that 80 percent of the employees aren't aligned with the company's culture of innovation? Are the employees unable to recognize innovation? Something's going wrong—it could be that the managers don't understand the program, but it could also be an early warning that the spirit of innovation has waned. That early warning can cause management to correct the problem long before the problem starts to hurt the bottom line. Alerted by this data, the division managers need to follow up and find the cause of the low numbers.

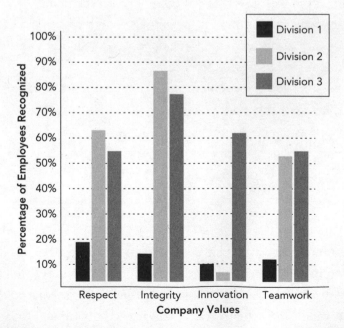

Figure 8.2 Departmental values distribution

Division 2 gives and receives many awards for the company values of respect and integrity, but few for innovation. It happens to be the accounting group, so this award profile is excellent.

Division 3 gives a high number of awards, balanced among all four values. This is good news for both the performance of the group (which should be cross-checked against other performance indicators) and for the group's use of the recognition program. The graph indicates strong engagement and high morale. This is the operations group, which happens to be a decentralized and disciplined department, capable of carrying on a recognition program without managers constantly reminding employees to participate.

An "early warning," incidentally, can also be a pleasant surprise. Imagine finding a spirit of innovation in unexpected places like the call center. Executives who discover hidden strengths from their dashboard data can capitalize on those strengths. If your customer service group is innovative, you might join that capability with sales and marketing efforts to increase customer satisfaction and "share of wallet."

Values distribution at the highest level can also differentiate how culture is practiced in different locations. The dashboard for a company with several large offices might look like Figure 8.3.

A glance at this dashboard shows that innovation is present and recognized throughout the company locations, with a greater count in the Americas corresponding to the larger employee numbers in those locations. Customer service and innovation are healthy globally. Low scores on teamwork and operational excellence across all locations are consequential and demand quick investigation.

As the name implies, dashboards indicate the performance across many systems and dimensions, just like the dashboard of a car. The really interesting stuff happens when you go beyond the metaphor and examine performance over time, as social recognition enables leaders—and employees—to direct and influence company culture.

Another dashboard analysis can show if the social recognition budget is working efficiently. Is it on budget? Is your spread of awards as you predicted in number and value? Here are two examples (Figures 8.4 and 8.5):

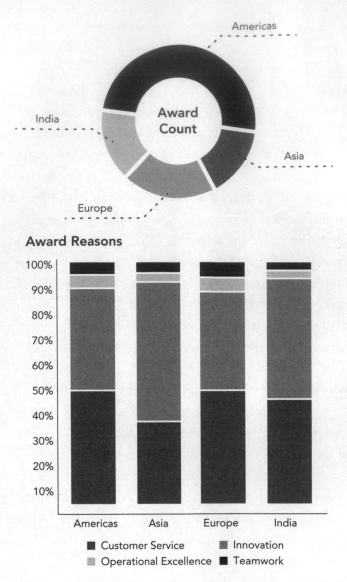

Figure 8.3 Geographic values distribution

These two charts show the number of awards given on the left and the amount of budget invested in those awards on the right. The optimal charts should form a valley when viewed side by side as illustrated in Figure 8.4.

The left side of this chart is descending, meaning that the program is designed to be meritocratic. The larger awards, which are far fewer in

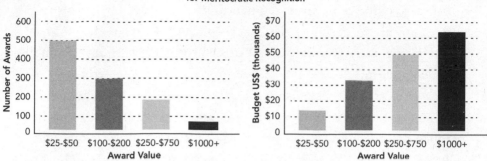

Figure 8.4 Proper budget distribution for meritocratic recognition

number than the lower-value awards, gravitate toward the more impactful instances of employee behavior. This indicates larger awards are going to those employees on the high end of the performance bell curve.

The ascending right side of the chart indicates that the greatest numbers of awards are lower in cost, and the program is fundamentally designed to maximize visibility and penetration. Simply put, the company has opted to make the program more inclusive while still distributing the few high-value awards to the highest-impact performers.

If these charts, viewed side-by-side, were to appear as in Figure 8.5, then the distribution indicates an elitist program focused mostly on the highest performers. With the largest number of awards being given at

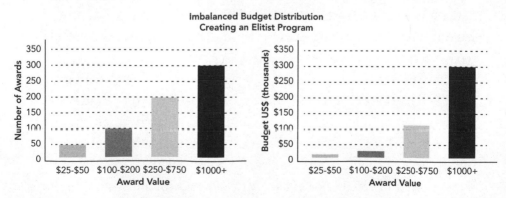

Figure 8.5 Imbalanced budget distribution creating an elitist program

the highest value, far fewer employees are recognized while the budget spent on recognition increases dramatically.

An executive can simply glance at these charts to assure the program is trending in the right direction. If it isn't, the early warning system is ringing an alarm.

These metrics are diagnostic and carry a powerful message that executive management cares about the program. Reports should go up the organization, ideally all the way to the CEO. This causes a cascade effect down the line; when everybody from the top down has a stake in hitting the goals, the clarity, urgency, and importance of the program magnifies. Everyone with authority is responsible. This cascade effect spreads learning through informal networks and through relationships with managers—the social architecture at work.

Summarizing the Case

We've listed the strategic value of social recognition throughout this book under the broad theme of making your company a better place to work, not only because it's the right thing to do, but also as a matter of self-interest. When you roll up the ROI case for implementing social recognition in a strategic framework, there are returns you can quantify immediately, as well as long-term returns on a recognition investment.

Immediately quantifiable are savings like lowered turnover; if you performed the turnover cost calculation (above) with your company's payroll numbers you have some idea of the hard-dollar value social recognition brings to the bottom line.

Over time, the value of a more engaged workforce accrues in many small and large ways, and their dollar value depends on the relative cost-versus-payoff numbers for different companies, industries, and cultures. For example, lowering safety incidents or raising quality might be the highest-value benefits to a manufacturer. A software firm might find the biggest benefit in higher productivity or reduced absenteeism. Working off Gallup's list from the beginning of this chapter, consider the value that higher engagement, enabled by social recognition, would provide for your company:

21 percent higher productivity means:

- Higher sales
- Faster innovation
- More new products
- More calls answered
- More projects completed on time and under budget

22 percent higher profitability means:

- More money for R&D
- Higher dividends for shareholders
- More money for employees in profit-sharing programs
- A higher profile in your industry
- More influence for senior leaders inside and outside the industry

41 percent higher quality (fewer defects) means:

- Happier customers
- Fewer replacement costs
- Lower inventory
- Reputational benefit
- A well-regarded brand inside and outside the industry

48 percent fewer safety incidents means:

- Happier employees
- Happier families
- Lower medical insurance costs
- Fewer OSHA reportable incidents and fines
- Higher productivity

- Less management time distracted by unnecessary safety issues
- Happier customers

37 percent reduced absenteeism means:

- Happier workers
- Happier families
- Happier CFOs

10 percent higher customer ratings means:

- More return customers (higher loyalty)
- More word-of-mouth and viral (unsolicited) marketing
- Less time/money spent resolving customer issues
- Pricing power versus lower-rated competitors

All of these make you more competitive in the marketplace because if you achieve all of these things, you are executing against strategy better than your competitors.

There are other areas where greater engagement through social recognition might be important to your company and your industry, and we encourage you to include them in your calculation of short-term and long-term benefit. For example, what would higher participation in service activities do to your corporate social responsibility (CSR) efforts? Would greater engagement lead to greater participation in training and education, and thus a more skilled workforce? How would directly recognizing individuals for innovation, perseverance, courage, and creativity benefit your company?

Through the Looking-Glass

Some of our customers like to consider the business case for social recognition from a different angle. They ask, what effect would *less* recognition produce? For example:

- Do we want to recognize our people less for acting out company values?
- Do we want a negativity-dominated workplace?
- Would talent acquisition be easier if we were thought of as a lousy place to work?
- Would higher turnover help the bottom line?

The answers are obvious.

A long time ago, when "labor" meant planting wheat and building pyramids, the most important qualities in a workforce were muscle and compliance. Later, basic physical skills and organization became the building blocks of a workforce. As the Industrial Age advanced, ever-greater physical skills and a more educated workforce meant competitive advantage globally.

Note the pattern: as civilization (and business) advanced, competitive advantage shifted from a workforce that emphasized physical ability and compliance to a workforce that emphasized mental ability and voluntary effort.

Today, what matters most in a workforce is mastery of advanced knowledge and discretionary effort to apply that effort in known and novel ways. High skills and strong culture produce the greatest return on investment in the workforce. The best business practices—and we adamantly include social recognition among those—encourage both from the moment a potential job candidate learns your company's name to the day an employee retires.

9 How Social Recognition Impacts HR

"We have a lot of engineers and they 'speak' data," says Corinne Selk, Organizational Development and Performance Specialist at IM Flash Technologies. "What's great about recognition data is that we are able to use it to measure aspects of our culture we previously couldn't get numbers around, like strategic behaviors and our company values."

Engineers like data, and in an engineering culture, even HR is expected to harness data.

Selk continues, "What's really great about the data we're able to get from social recognition is that we can link it to other HR metrics we track like engagement, attraction, and retention. And because we're a very execution-driven company, it's important that we are able to see how effectively recognition is driving our talent management outcomes, and ultimately our business results."

* * *

We are in the early stages of a pervasive technological movement grouped under the umbrella term "big data." Huge sets of data are examined by powerful analytic tools at unimaginable speeds to generate insights about the past and present, and even to predict the future (a practice called predictive analytics). You already see the effects of this nascent movement: Weather forecasts are more accurate. Marketers detect trends before they are obvious and create products to serve those trends. Retailers stock shelves with just enough products to meet demand. Web pages contain eerily personal advertising.

Big data is working its way into talent management as advanced HR systems mine data of all kinds to make informed predictions about, for example, which employees are most productive and why, which valuable employees are "flight risks" (in time to do something about the situation), and who might be a great succession candidate for a key position.

In Chapter 5, we said that insight was the final step in the recognition journey. Management always seeks to understand the interactions of behavior, information, knowledge, and emotion that result in success or failure. These interactions are incredibly complex in a large modern organization, and they are always imperfect, which is why insight is so valuable. Once you understand how something really works—a process, a product, a human chain of emotion—you can more readily harness it to accomplish your goals.

Data analysis has long been used to understand complex physical processes—a great example is the revolution in inventory management and "just in time" delivery that has transformed manufacturing in the last 40 years. By analyzing where components had to be, when, and how many, manufacturers of complicated products from automobiles to microchips held costs down and sped up productivity.

HR has had a smaller but important taste of modern data analysis in recent decades with the advent of human capital management (HCM) software for payroll and benefits management, compensation analysis, cost containment, and other practices. It has been able to help measure outcomes of programs like employee wellness initiatives. Adoption has been slow, however, compared to other practices. According to Aberdeen Group Research, "only 30 percent of organizations combine talent data with business data to measure the impact on organizational performance."[1] The opportunities presented in merging talent data with business data are hard to overstate.

*Social recognition's data and practices advance
HR with talent insight.*

Social recognition's data and practices advance HR with talent insight across the HCM life cycle, from the moment a candidate encounters a company, through the hiring process, and during a career. The illustration from Gartner[2] in Figure 9.1 neatly captures the ways in which that works:

At the top of Figure 9.1, for example, we see a relationship between continuous feedback and performance management. It's well known that effective managers provide continuous feedback to employees. Just so, continuous feedback from social recognition helps an employee focus on the most important activities (in addition to other benefits we've described as the power of thanks). Furthermore, capturing continuous feedback in a social recognition system enables managers to

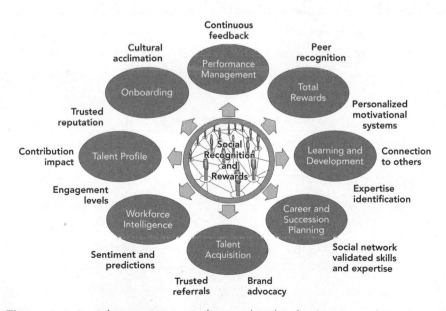

Figure 9.1 Social recognition and reward technologies are reshaping traditional talent management processes

give more accurate performance reviews. And relating that feedback to performance enables HR and other executives to understand which activities, methods, and knowledge result in the best performance.

At the bottom of the illustration, we can see that trusted referrals and (employer) brand advocacy help in talent acquisition. Trusted referrals happen when employees invest their relationship capital—their networks—into a company they like and respect. It is a natural extension of thanks. Those who make referrals can be recognized and rewarded, and patterns emerge in the data. For example, a global organization could spot "super referral sources"—employees who bring in many successful candidates—in any corner of the globe. Imagine convening a group of these employees from around the world to refine recruiting messages, referral programs, and related activities! You can only do this when you can positively identify those people, which in a large organization is now much easier, thanks to broad data analysis.

As for branding, employee recognition is a formal component of earning public accolades as an exceptional place to work, and the company becomes more attractive to candidates. This in turn raises the quality of applicants and lowers the cost of recruiting.

So it is with each of the eight talent management processes described in the illustration: social recognition and reward technologies enhance each process with fact-based feedback and yield data that can be analyzed for insights into virtually every human activity in an organization.

Getting Through Tough Times

The business cycle forces a dilemma on every chief human resources officer from time to time. You see it often in small companies in a growth stage and in large companies when they hit a rough patch due to a weak economy. The dilemma is this: just at the time when they need most to build morale and sustain the culture to weather hard times, the money dries up. Merit increases are cancelled. Bonuses are cut back or postponed, or even stopped. Morale hits the floor because it's such a difficult environment, made even more frightening if employees witness layoffs. Maintaining and encouraging discretionary effort seems like an impossible task.

Recognition is a good place to start. For a fraction of the cost of a typical bonus program, companies can still show appreciation and make the most of fewer budget dollars. One percent of payroll, magnified by 10,000 heartfelt messages of appreciation, can do wonders for engagement in the stressed-out workforce.

Benefits of Talent Insight

In the past, these insights might come from a particularly sensitive manager or HR professional, but in a large organization there are just too many people and too much activity for a single observer to reliably detect hidden patterns. That's the power of big data analysis—it observes far more than a person can and, with the sheer power to run large data sets, it observes patterns that might otherwise go unnoticed.

A sophisticated social recognition program can show these patterns. When you analyze many thousands of recognition moments and comments, you can produce key insights about how jobs get done, how teams should be configured, how communication and learning and collaboration happen across the hall and around the globe, and where to find your company's "hidden influencers"—that is, people who might not wield formal power but who are so trusted and widely known that their opinion carries great weight with peers.

In a global organization, this kind of analysis crosses borders as well. Analytics can spot employees who live certain values in exceptional ways no matter where they work: for example, pinpointing an employee in

Brazil who is passionate about innovation, speaks Portuguese, English, and German, and would be perfect for an upcoming role in Europe.

Big data is also enabling insight to travel horizontally within HR functions, contributing to recruitment, hiring, retention, and compensation and benefits planning. Social recognition data is particularly interesting in its implications for performance management.[3]

Here are 14 ways social recognition and the data it yields contribute to broader talent management practices:

Onboarding: One surefire way to help new employees ramp up quickly—internalizing your values and jumping feet first into your culture—is to nominate and appreciate their work, and to invite them to notice and recognize their peers for doing great work. Immediate feedback from social recognition in the critical three to six months after a new employee starts helps new employees to understand how their work and their efforts align with company values and contribute to company goals.

Finding hidden value: The technology of social recognition delivers feedback data to executive management by capturing individual moments of great performance. The resulting company-wide recognition story reveals pockets of excellence that might otherwise go unnoticed. When a manager recognizes "unsung heroes," those heroes are motivated *and* the recognition of their behavior motivates others.

Documenting and promoting best practices: As a social recognition program captures incremental improvements in processes of all kinds through recognition awards, those improvements can be collected and published to all in a continuous stream of best practices.

Spotting the quiet but important employees: When recognition events produce meaningful data and that data is captured, senior management can identify "hidden influencers"—that is, employees with large and active internal networks. Those who are recognized for continuous improvement, for example, are certainly high-potential employees, whether they work in the research lab or on the loading dock. Over time, recognition singles out both the "popular" employees and those too modest or shy to promote themselves, but whose work inspires others and produces results.

Spotting "cultural energizers": At the other end of the scale are employees who constantly energize the culture with enthusiasm, inclusiveness, curiosity, ethical example, perseverance, a will to win, or any of the other qualities that express a culture. They will give recognition and often receive it, and they are key allies for cultural initiatives, whether that means managing change or instituting a recognition program in the first place.

Learning and development: It is hard to overstate the role of recognition as a way to reinforce a culture of learning in an organization. Because recognition is a pure form of positive reinforcement, it can serve to help bolster any behavior your organization values. In fact, when scholars of organizational behavior identified the top drivers of learning on the job, reward was one of the most important factors, and one of the top hindering elements was a lack of positive reinforcement.

Retention: One of the most measurable and quantifiable effects that companies see from recognition is a jump in retention numbers—and the huge cost savings that accompanies it. Our Workforce Mood Tracker surveys have shown that employees will consider jumping ship for a company that recognizes and rewards employees. A study by Bersin by Deloitte noted that "companies with recognition programs highly effective at improving employee engagement have 31 percent lower voluntary turnover than their peers with ineffective recognition programs."[4]

Change management: One of the lesser-known impacts of a great recognition program is its ability to ease change management in an organization. Whether it is something as large as a merger or acquisition or as simple as new processes and ideas, recognition is a way to reinforce new behavior and make everyone feel like an important stakeholder in company culture. Recognition brings even the most resistant or disparate groups together into a single culture focused on a single set of goals and values. Moreover, positive reinforcement is proven to be a powerful driver of behavioral change.

Succession planning: Good succession planning has multiple benefits. It lowers recruitment cost while at the same time making employees feel great about their chances for advancement and their future in the organization. It enables smoother transitions as management openings are filled from within, putting in place someone already familiar with company culture and goals. Because social recognition locates high performers, quiet-but-important employees, and cultural energizers, it helps HR build a deep bench for the company's future.

Years-of-service awards: In Chapter 5, we described a reimagining of the old-fashioned, traditional years-of-service award. The stories collected in a social years-of-service award are both quantitative and qualitative; saving them enables a company to create and share a narrative of engaged, passionate employees and the strong relations that carry a company beyond the tenure and vision of its founders. Capturing data over the long term means a years-of-service milestone can present a review of every time someone has been congratulated, recognized, or thanked—a personal record of someone's significance, which is so much more important than someone's longevity. A years-of-service timeline, containing heartfelt thanks and shared widely, radiates good feeling and human appreciation throughout the organization.

Work circles: In the cadence of today's workplace, people form "Work circles™," a term we use to describe the mini-communities that form around a project instead of an organizational chart. They might be temporary or long-term relationships, and they aren't restricted to a single department or location. At any time, an employee might belong to several work circles because he or she is engaged in projects that require different arrays of skills and different resources. Writing this book, for example, involved people from different parts of Globoforce (executive, creative, marketing, strategy and consulting services, research, product management, and communications), all focused on the objective of creating the book. That's a work circle. People in a company who otherwise might not have much contact became a self-sustaining, self-regulating group, and their collaboration became a little part of each individual's work history.

Recognition moments among them capture some of that unique experience, and anyone with access to the recognition data can learn about the skills, temperament, and engagement of individual team members long after the work circle disbands because the book is finished. The storytelling of each person's tenure in this company can be retained by a social recognition system that recognizes the unique relationships and can be instantly generated as an individual work digest. That just wasn't possible in the past, and even if someone wanted to create it, the burden of research and storytelling on HR would be prohibitive.

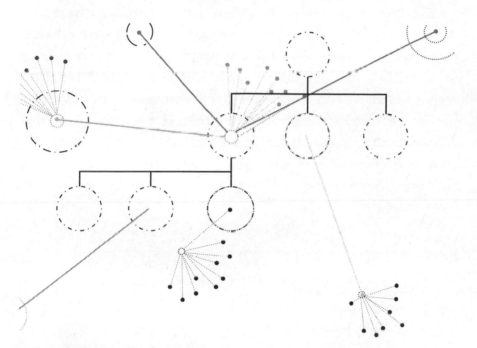

Figure 9.2 Work circles

Identifying management trouble spots: Social recognition can also reveal gaps in management performance. For example, if no recognition takes place in a department delivering on its goals, that data point could mean the manager isn't noticing or appreciating employee performance, which is an early warning sign of such problems as employee turnover. If, on the other hand, a manager is handing out a lot of recognition awards but not hitting goals, the data suggest that employees aren't focused on the right outcomes.

Improving performance reviews: A social recognition program provides rich qualitative and quantitative information for performance reviews.

At the simplest level, recognition records outstanding performance that deserves to be remembered at review time. At its most sophisticated, data-rich social recognition revolutionizes performance management with the *crowdsourced performance review.* This is a concept so powerful that Eric has written a separate book describing what it is, how it works, and why it's an HR management tool whose time has come.[5]

Separating quality from quantity: Qualitative recognition data records the value of certain behaviors and accomplishments. This is critical when many awards are being given, because quantity is not the only measure of value. This is especially valuable in large web-based systems and aligns with the social behavior you already practice on the web. HR has experienced the "paradox of abundance" in recruiting, where the system that delivers the most résumés is not necessarily the best system. Likewise, an effective recognition system can single out employees who might receive few awards, but those awards collectively represent the greatest value to the company.

The Crowdsourced Performance Review

The traditional performance review is cumbersome, riddled with weak points, and out of date. The Crowdsourced Performance Review (CPR) is a complementary practice that remedies those weaknesses. In a nutshell, CPR proposes that, in addition to a manager judging an individual's performance, everyone in the organization with whom that person works has input into his or her performance on a regular, spontaneous basis. By recording an unlimited number of instances when an employee demonstrates good work, and mapping his or her behavior and relationships around the organization, social recognition produces a rich narrative of any employee's behavior, influence, and accomplishments. Manager, employee, and executives can thus assess a real-time, fact-based performance record.

Predicting the Future

Predicting performance is one of the great, elusive goals of human resources. The point of every job interview is to anticipate with accuracy how someone will perform, and whenever someone is promoted, the organization is placing a bet on that employee to thrive in a new position. If human beings could only be as predictable as machines, HR would have a much simpler job.

But human beings, in all their complexity and variety, are the focus of HR practices, and so HR is always looking for better ways to understand and predict employee behavior.

We are just beginning to see real data solutions to this in social recognition. Based on the belief that past behavior can predict future behavior (the belief that underlies behavior-based interviewing, for example), analysis of social recognition data can and does help predict performance.

When we talk to customers in large organizations, we find there are departments and leaders that lead the way with successful social recognition and get valuable insights all the time. When they dig deeply into the data, they also find unexpected insights of a predictive nature. For example, they may see that recognition activity in a certain manager's department happens because his or her influence reflects popularity and good feeling but is ultimately not connected to business results. That can be corrected, but it also has implications for that manager's ultimate career path. Put recognition data against business data, and you can predict that turnover of a certain type of employee will increase when a new manager is put in charge. You can anticipate which individuals are contributing well but will ultimately fall by the wayside. You can predict which individual experts might become good managers and which should remain individual contributors—all this based on real-time recognition of qualities like leadership, teamwork, and alignment with company values, combined with outcomes like improved quality, higher productivity, and higher profits.

Will predictive analytics ultimately make 100 percent accurate calls on who should work at what, where, and with whom in an organization?

Human beings have a talent for defying predictions, and so "predicting the future of prediction" is a dicey business. But creating a perfect crystal ball is impossible. People will always surprise you with their capacity to grow and change.

The job of human resources is to manage practices that make the most of every person in the organization. Predictive analytics and social recognition are tools to help HR professionals do their jobs. And those tools are getting better all the time.

AFTERWORD

There's a question we get asked when we meet customers for the first time. It's a question that should be asked of any company that claims to innovate across an entire business sector: "Do you drink your own champagne? Does Globoforce spend its money on a full-featured social recognition practice?"

Yes, it does. Our social recognition program is called Globostars. Everyone participates. When you walk into our offices, you'll see the Globostars awards feed on a big screen, calling out the latest employees to be recognized for living our company values. That's the obvious sign we're true believers.

But there's an even more public sign of our commitment to the principles in this book. Globoforce was named to several lists of best places to work in both Europe and North America. The Great Place to Work® Institute ranked us number 3 in Ireland, among the Top 50 in Europe, and number 25 in our category in the United States. Two years ago, the *Boston Globe* named Globoforce the number one workplace in our category in Massachusetts (our U.S. home).

That would be gratifying for any company, but it's extraordinary for us because we are a relatively small, fast, high-growth company with limited resources. We constantly remind ourselves that we're not Google, with a fire hydrant of free cash flow that could, theoretically, throw money around at everyone.

In a start-up and fast-growth environment, nobody has all the resources they want; nobody gets all the training they deserve—not because these aren't good things, but because resources have to be managed with great care. There isn't much margin for error. Every available resource goes into improving the product, into marketing, into providing great service to customers. And in the great tradition of shoemaker's children, we, as an HR tech company, just can't spend much money on big bonuses or perquisites.

But we do have the best social recognition program we can build, and everyone in the company participates. And Globostars is the reason that objective third parties name Globoforce as a great workplace. It's enabled us to create a deep culture of recognition globally. It's a cultural amplifier, boosting affinity for the company and each other and daily reinforcing the right behaviors. It's one of the only tools we have to manage culture, and it's delivered a gratifying endorsement of what we're trying to achieve with those best place to work awards.

But much more than outside applause, our program and our culture of recognition has made Globoforce *feel* like a great workplace. Lynette Silva, a member of this book's work circle, says about that feeling, "our blood runs Globoforce blue."

We wish the same for your company—that social recognition and the Power of Thanks makes your company a best place to work. They will surely make it a very successful place to work. The people who show up every day to live your mission and values, who put so much of their lives into working together under your company name, deserve no less.

NOTES

Introduction
1. Adam Bryant, "Planes, Cars and Cathedrals," Corner Office, *New York Times*, September 5, 2009, http://www.nytimes.com/2009/09/06/business/06corner.html?_r=1&pagewanted=2.

Chapter 1
1. Frances Frei and Anne Morriss, "Culture Takes Over When the CEO Leaves the Room," Harvard Business Review Blog Network, May 10, 2012, http://blogs.hbr.org/2012/05/culture-takes-over-when-the-ce/.
2. June 16, 2009, http://blog.threestarleadership.com/2009/06/22/home-depot-at-30-a-lesson-in-corporate-culture.aspx.
   June 22, 2009, http://blog.threestarleadership.com/2009/06/16/lessons-from-the-rise-and-fall-of-delta-airlines.aspx.
3. Louis V. Gerstner, Jr., *Who Says Elephants Can't Dance?* (New York, HarperBusiness 2002).
4. The full One Ford document—a single page—may be found at http://corporate.ford.com/doc/one_ford.pdf.
5. http://www.mckinsey.com/insights/strategy/leading_in_the_21st_century_an_interview_with_fords_alan_mulally
6. Towers Watson / WorldatWork 2012–2013 Global Talent Management and Rewards Study, http://www.worldatwork.org/waw/adimLink?id=71255.
7. Paul Meehan, Orit Gadiesh, and Shintaro Hori, "Culture As a Competitive Advantage," Bain & Co. Executive Forum, Winter 2006.
8. Frei and Morriss, op. cit.

Chapter 2
1. "The Number One Job Skill in 2020," June 11, 2013, http://www.linkedin.com/today/post/article/20130611180041-59549-the-no-1-job-skill-in-2020.
2. William James, *The Letters of William James: Volume 2*, ed. Henry James (1920).
3. ADP-ES, The Workforce View in 2013. Full report available at http://www.adp-es.co.uk/assets/vfs/Account-51143/workforceview2013/ADP-infographic-Workforce-view-2013.pdf.
4. Leigh Branham, "Why Managers Fail to Recognize Employee Contributions," Globoforce Blog, February 18, 2013 http://www.globoforce.com/gfblog/2013/why-managers-fail-to-recognize-employee-contributions/.
5. Steve Kerr, *Reward Systems: Does Yours Measure Up?* (Harvard Business Review Press, 2008).
6. http://www.huffingtonpost.com/2014/06/03/us-children-emotional-physical-abuse_n_5440277.html

7. One example: A. M. Isen, K. D. Aubman, and G. P. Nowicki, "Positive Affect Facilitates Creative Problem Solving," *Journal of Personality and Social Psychology* 52 (1987): 1122–1131.

8. Engagement's power to improve financial results is well documented. For a recent example see Aon Hewitt's *2013 Trends in Employee Engagement*, http://www.aon .com/human-capital-consulting/thought-leadership/talent_mgmt/2013_Trends_in_ Global_Employee_Engagement.jsp.

9. Tony Hsieh, *Delivering Happiness: A Path to Profits, Passion and Purpose* (New York: Grand Central Publishing, 2013).

10. David Marquet, *Turn the Ship Around! A True Story of Turning Followers into Leaders* (New York, Portfolio, 2013).

11. Who won? Both—the videos were funny and upbeat, the producer was quickly hired by another firm, and the company got great publicity.

Chapter 3

1. Roy F. Baumeister, Kathleen D. Vohs, Jennifer L. Aaker, and Emily N. Garbinsky, "Some Key Differences Between a Happy Life and a Meaningful Life," forthcoming in *Journal of Positive Psychology*.

2. *Ibid.*

3. The information in this section appears in a different form in Eric's book *The Crowdsourced Performance Review*.

4. Alexandra Levit with Sanja Licina, "How the Recession Shaped Millennial and Hiring Manager Attitudes About Millennials' Future Careers," commissioned by the Career Advisory Board, 2011.

5. Interview with Thad Peterson, "Givers: The Key to Organizational Effectiveness," http://www.globoforce.com/resources/features/givers-the-key-to-organizational-effectiveness/.(No date).

6. This list is assembled from numerous surveys. For a full citation of research behind this list, see Darcy Jacobson's article at http://www.globoforce.com/gfblog/2013/ the-power-of-workplace-gratitude-a-brief-bibliography/.

7. Adam M. Grant and Francesca Gino, "A Little Thanks Goes a Long Way: Explaining Why Gratitude Expressions Motivate Prosocial Behavior, *Journal of Personality and Social Psychology* 98, no. 6 (June 2010), 946–955.

8. This is right in our DNA. Recent studies have focused on more primitive but very real versions of these needs in other mammals, such as primates. See Charles Siebert, *The Wauchula Woods Accord: Toward a New Understanding of Animals* (Scribner, 2009).

9. In what is called Herzberg's "two-factor" theory, he differentiated what he called hygiene factors (working conditions, salary and status, company policy and benefits, and working relationships) from motivation factors (recognition, achievements, level of responsibility, and need for personal growth). Hygiene factors promote job satisfaction, and motivation factors promote motivation.

10. See Stephen R. Covey, *The Seven Habits of Highly Effective People*, pp. 190–203. New York, Free Press, Revised edition 2004

11. Adecco Group North America, *American Insights Workplace Survey*, Melville, New York 2009.

12. Tom Rath and Donald O. Clifton, *How Full Is Your Bucket?* (New York, Gallup Press, 2004).

13. Martin Dewhurst, Matthew Guthridge, and Elizabeth Mohr, "Motivating People: Getting Beyond Money," *McKinsey Quarterly*, November 2009.

14. Teresa Amabile and Steven Kramer, *The Progress Principle: Using Small Wins to Ignite Joy, Engagement, and Creativity at Work* (Watertown, MA: Harvard Business Review Press, 2011).
15. Towers Watson, *Engagement at Risk: Driving Strong Performance in a Volatile Global Environment*, 2012. (http://www.towerswatson.com/assets/pdf/2012-Towers-Watson-Global-Workforce-Study.pdf)
16. *The Power of Three: Taking Engagement to New Heights*, Towers Watson Perspectives, 2013. (http://www.towerswatson.com/en-US/Insights/IC-Types/Survey-Research-Results/2011/02/The-Power-of-Three--Taking-Engagement-to-New-Heights)
17. Tony Schwartz and Catherine McCarthy, "Manage Your Energy, Not Your Time," *Harvard Business Review*, October 2007. The authors are respectively president and founder and senior vice president of The Energy Project, a business consultancy.

Chapter 4
1. Steve Lohr, "At Last, a Sneak Preview of Big Blue's Strategy," *New York Times*, March 24, 1994.
2. Lisa DiCarlo, "How Lou Gerstner Got IBM to Dance," *Forbes*, November 11, 2002.
3. Alan Murray, *The Wall Street Journal Essential Guide to Management: Lasting Lessons from the Best Leadership Minds of Our Time* (New York, HarperCollins Business, 2010). Adapted from "How to Change Your Organization's Culture" from the *Wall Street Journal*'s Lessons in Leadership.
4. State of the American Workplace, Gallup, 2012.
5. Glenn Rifkin, obituary of Amar G. Bose, *New York Times*, July 12, 2013.
6. For a detailed critique of stack ranking, see *The Crowdsourced Performance Review*.
7. Jack Welch with Suzy Welch, *Winning* (HarperBusiness, 2005), http://www.welchway.com/Principles/Differentiation.aspx.
8. "The Secret Ingredient in GE's Talent-Review System," HBR Blog Network, April 17, 2014.
9. At a Society of Human Resources conference, Hsieh told a story about how he called the Zappos customer service line pretending that he got the wrong number as he meant to call a pizza shop. The customer service rep helped him out with the pizza order.
10. "The Zappos Way of Managing," *Inc.* magazine, May 1, 2009, http://www.inc.com/magazine/20090501/the-zappos-way-of-managing.html.
11. "Making Sure the Shoe Fits at Zappos.com," *New York Times*, November 6, 2008.
12. Interview with Globoforce, May 6, 2014.
13. "Culture's Most Important Ingredient," Piver, Susan. Globoforce Blog September 13, 2013.

Chapter 5
1. From this webinar: http://player.vimeo.com/video/33762135.
2. Interview with Globoforce's Kerry Murphy, April 13, 2014.
3. *Adapting to the Realities of our Changing Workforce*, Globoforce Workforce Mood Tracker™, Spring 2014 report.
4. From Globoforce webinar, "Your Engagement Survey Is Done. Now What?" with Mary Ann Masarech, BlessingWhite.

Chapter 6
1. Yvette Cameron, "Social Employee Recognition Systems Reward the Business with Results," Gartner, December 2013.

2. Andy Molinsky, *Global Dexterity: How to Adapt Your Behavior Across Cultures Without Losing Yourself in the Process* (Watertown, MA: Harvard Business Review Press, 2013).
3. Susan A. Murphy, "Leading a Multigenerational Workforce," AARP, 2007. Several statements about generational attitudes are based on this report.
4. Interview with Kerry Murphy of Globoforce, April 13, 2014.
5. Jim Lundy, "Drive Employee Performance with Social Recognition," Aragon Research Notes Number 2013-35, October 4, 2013.
6. Leonard A. Schlesinger, Charles F. Kiefer, and Paul B. Brown, *Just Start: Take Action, Embrace Uncertainty, Create the Future* (Boston: Harvard Business Review Press, 2012).
7. Eric Pfanner, "Mobile Devices Overtake PC Sales at Lenovo," *New York Times*, August 15, 2013.
8. "Smartphone Explosion in 2014 Will See Ownership in India Pass US," *The Guardian*, January 13, 2014.
9. Adobe 2013 Mobile Consumer Survey.
10. "Reports from vendors indicate that more than 80% of their overall HCM new business is coming from SaaS on a global basis across all employee size segments.... Of those global enterprises that choose to replace their core HRMS, a strong majority are choosing SaaS over traditional on-premises or hosted ERP, and we expect that trend will continue to gain momentum in 2014." Gartner, 2014 review of 2011 Prediction, cited in "Predicts 2014: Nexus Forces Redefine Human Capital Management."
11. "Forget Work-Life Balance: It's Time for Work-Life Blend" Ron Ashkenas, Forbes, October 19, 2012
12. Teresa Amabile and Steven Kramer, *The Progress Principle: Using Small Wins to Ignite Joy, Engagement, and Creativity at Work* (Boston: Harvard Business Review Press, 2011).
13. See http://www.slideshare.net/dings/95-theses-on-the-power-and-efficacy-of-gamification-14625326.
14. Emma Snider, "In Social Recognition Systems, Watch the Gamification Elements," TechTarget, http://searchfinancialapplications.techtarget.com/tip/In-social-recognition-systems-watch-the-gamification-elements.

Chapter 7

1. Towers Watson (formally Towers Perrin) 2007–2008 Global Workforce Study.
2. See http://www.aon.com/human-capital-consulting/thought-leadership/talent_mgmt/2013_Trends_in_Global_Employee_Engagement.jsp.
3. "Predicts 2014: Nexus Forces Redefine Human Capital Management," Gartner, December 2013, https://www.gartner.com/doc/2631840/predicts--nexus-forces-redefine.
4. *Trends in Employee Recognition*, WorldatWork, June 2013.
5. Globoforce Workforce MoodTracker™ Survey Fall 2012.
6. Ibid.
7. "Employee Recognition at Intuit," Stanford Graduate School of Business, Case HR-31, March 10, 2008.
8. "Reward and Recognition Program Profiles and Best Practices 2008," Ascent Group.

Chapter 8

1. Gallup, "State of the Global Workplace Report 2013," 21.
2. Edmans, Alex. "Does the Stock Market Fully Value Intangibles? Employee Satisfaction and Equity Prices" Research paper, Wharton School, University of Pennsylvania, July 31, 2009.

3. Jim Harter and Frank L. Schmidt, "What Really Drives Financial Success?," *Gallup Business Journal*, September 2, 2010.

4. Numerous studies conclude this; for an example see The Hay Group study announced at http://www.haygroup.com/ie/press/details.aspx?id=27599.

5. ROI (%) = (Gain from investment − cost of investment) / cost of investment × 100. So in this example, $8.2M - $4M = $4.2M $4.2M / $4M = 1.05 1.05 × 100 = 105% return on investment. (Thanks to Sarah Major, University of Georgia.)

6. Source: "100 best" data provided by Great Place to Work ® Institute, Inc. Comparative data provided by BLS. "100 Best" data include full-time and part-time turnover; BLS data include the same in addition to turnover for temp/contract workers. Where specified, ranges reflect data from different industries.

7. http://www.greatplacetowork.com/publications-and-events/blogs-and-news/2549-3-benefits-of-being-named-to-the-list.

8. FORTUNE/CNN estimates that in 2012 Google received more than 2 million applications and hired 8,064. http://tech.fortune.cnn.com/2012/02/24/google-recruiting/.

9. Hickman, Arvind, "IHG HRD: Employer brand is secret to success," HR Magazine [U.K.] January 20, 2014.

10. Hay Group Employee Engagement and Effectiveness Survey http://atrium.haygroup.com/us/our-products/employee-effectiveness-benefits.aspx.

11. Crowley, Mark C., "The Proof is in the Profits: America's Happiest Companies Make More Money," *Fast Company*, February 22, 2013 (update April 2014: even after the Spring 2014 market drop, Parnassus consistently has topped the S&P since this article was written).

12. Edmans, Alex (2011): "Does the Stock Market Fully Value Intangibles? Employee Satisfaction and Equity Prices." *Journal of Financial Economics* 101(3), 621–640.

13. Gartner, "Social Employee Recognition Systems Reward the Business with Results" 6 December 2013.

Chapter 9

1. Madeline Laurano, *Talent Analytics: Moving Beyond the Hype*, Aberdeen Group, April 2014.

2. Yvette Cameron, Gartner, *Social Employee Recognition Systems Reward the Business with Results*, December 6, 2013, https://www.gartner.com/doc/2634019/social-employee-recognition-systems-reward.

3. As described in Eric's 2013 book, *The Crowdsourced Performance Review*.

4. Stacia Garr, *The State of Employee Recognition 2012*, Bersin by Deloitte, June 11, 2012, http://www.bersin.com/practice/Detail.aspx?id=15539.

5. Mosley, Eric, *The Crowdsourced Performance Review* (New York, McGraw-Hill Professional, 2013).

INDEX

ABOUT THE AUTHORS

Eric Mosley

As cofounder and CEO of Globoforce, Eric Mosley has been directing the path of Globoforce as the innovator in the employee recognition industry since the company's beginning. His vision to raise recognition from a tactical, unmeasured, and undervalued effort to a global, social, and strategic program with clear measures for performance and success is now being realized in some of the world's largest and most complex organizations. Eric continues to shape the vision of innovation for the company and the industry.

As a recognized industry leader, Eric has personally advised some of the largest and most admired companies in the world. His insights has been published in such leading publications as *Fast Company*, *Forbes*, *Fortune*, *Harvard Business Review*, *The Sunday Times*, and *Time* magazine, and he has presented at industry and investment conferences across the world. Eric is also the author of the recently released McGraw-Hill title, *The Crowdsourced Performance Review*.

Derek Irvine

As Vice President, Client Strategy and Consulting at Globoforce, Derek leads the company's strategy and consulting division. In this role, he helps clients, including some of world's most admired companies, leverage proven recognition strategies and best practices to elevate employee engagement, increase retention, and improve bottom-line results. Derek is one of the world's foremost experts on employee recognition and engagement, helping business leaders worldwide set a higher vision and ambition for their company culture. As a renowned speaker and author of the acclaimed blog Recognize This!, he teaches HR and business leaders how to use recognition to proactively manage company culture. His viewpoints and writings are also regularly featured across major HR publications including *Workspan*, *HR Magazine*, *Human Resources Executive*, *Talent Management*, and *Workforce Management*.